The Pocket Encyclopaedia of World Aircraft in Colour

FIGHTERS

ATTACK AND TRAINING AIRCRAFT

1939-45

The Pocket Encyclopaedia
of World Aircraft in Colour

FIGHTERS

ATTACK AND TRAINING AIRCRAFT
1939–45

by
KENNETH MUNSON

Illustrated by
JOHN W. WOOD
Norman Dinnage
Frank Friend
Brian Hiley
William Hobson
Tony Mitchell
Jack Pelling

LONDON
BLANDFORD PRESS

First Published in 1969
Copyright © 1969 Blandford Press Ltd.

Colour printed by The Ysel Press, Deventer, Holland
Text printed and books bound in England
by Richard Clay (The Chaucer Press) Ltd.,
Bungay, Suffolk

PREFACE

So many different types of aeroplane, old and new, conventional and bizarre, were involved in the war of 1939–45 that any selection for a volume of this size must necessarily be an arbitrary one. In this initial presentation, therefore, the selection has been governed primarily by the operational importance of the aircraft concerned, although some types have other claims for inclusion.

As before, our collective thanks are due to Ian D. Huntley for his invaluable specific knowledge and general guidance in the matter of aircraft colouring and markings. Also of considerable assistance have been the three invaluable volumes of *Markings and Camouflage Systems of Luftwaffe Aircraft in World War II*, by Karl Ries Jr. Grateful acknowledgment is also made of items published at various times by *The Aeromodeller, AiReview, Air Pictorial, Aviation Magazine International*, the *Journal of the American Aviation Historical Society, Flying Review International, Interconair*, the *IPMS Magazine* and Profile Publications Ltd. Individual help was again kindly given by Lt.-Col. N. Kindberg of the Royal Swedish Air Force, and Jørgen Lundø of Politikens Forlag, Copenhagen. Finally, my thanks go, as always, to Pamela Matthews for her considerable help in the preparation and checking of the manuscript.

Kenneth Munson

June 1969

INTRODUCTION

The middle and late 1930s were years of considerable activity among the world's major aeronautical powers. Apart from the natural process of evolution of the military aeroplane, the advent of Adolf Hitler's National Socialist party to power in Germany, and the increasing strength of the new *Luftwaffe* that followed, led many nations to realise – some less quickly than others – that policies of 'making do' with their air forces' existing equipment for another year or two were extremely unwise. Thus, most of the leading nations in Europe embarked at this time upon schemes for the expansion and re-equipment of their air forces with more modern combat types. Even so, at the time of the outbreak of World War 2 none could yet match the *Luftwaffe* either in numerical strength or in the modernity of its equipment.

The restrictions imposed upon Germany in 1919 by the Treaty of Versailles had included a categorical ban on the manufacture of all but a modest output of light civil aircraft. But with the signing of the Paris Air Agreement seven years later most of the former restrictions were removed, and from this point there began, even before Hitler, the gradual re-establishment of a healthy aviation industry, with factories set up in such countries as Switzerland and the USSR as well as in Germany itself. New military aircraft began to appear, in the early 1930s, ostensibly as 'fast mailplanes', 'sporting single-seaters' and the like for the national airline, Deutsche Lufthansa, or for the re-created *Luftsportverband*, a supposed private flying organisation which was actually turning out military pilots for the new *Luftwaffe*. The practice of allocating civilian registration letters to new prototypes was but the thinnest of disguises for aircraft whose military purpose was all too readily apparent. Little further attempt was made to preserve the fiction after Hitler's accession to power in 1933, and the existence of the *Luftwaffe* was confirmed officially by the German government in 1935. Indicative of the rate at which this air force expanded thereafter is the fact that, at the end of 1935, the industry's output of aircraft was some three hundred a month; by September 1939 it was in excess of a thousand a month.

Germany's eventual ally of the European war, Italy, also embarked upon a re-equipment programme – though by comparison a much more modest one – after the conclusion of its campaigns in Abyssinia during the mid-1930s. But whereas Germany, for its new generations of both fighters and bombers, was clearly pinning its faith on the monoplane, Italy, so far as fighters at least were concerned, was reluctant to eschew the biplanes that had served the *Regia Aeronautica* so well for so long. This reflects the somewhat different conception of the ideal fighting machine held by Italian pilots since the days of World War 1: twenty years later, these airmen still preferred the open cockpit and the lightly armed machine in which outright speed took second place to the ability to out-manoeuvre its opponents.

The Spanish Civil War of 1936–39 afforded several of the major air powers, Germany and Italy among them, an apparently ideal opportunity to try out their new range of military aeroplanes under genuine battle conditions. The ensuing campaigns undoubtedly provided useful experience not only in the evaluation of existing combat types but in drawing attention to future tactical requirements. (For example, it was the Spanish campaigns that led German officials to realise the need for specialised ground-attack aircraft, a realisation that led to the appearance of the Henschel Hs 129 in this role during World War 2.) On the other hand, the aircrews of Germany's *Legion Condor* and Italy's *Aviazione Legionaria* in Spain were so often pitted against markedly inferior opposition that the efficacy of their own aircraft was somewhat over-estimated by world standards.

The peacetime expansion of the RAF during the immediate pre-war years was, by comparison, modest and slow, despite the augmented output resulting from the 'shadow factory' programme, in which the British motor-car industry turned out components or complete aeroplanes to supplement those produced by the recognised aircraft manufacturers. Like Italy, Britain was reluctant to sound the death-knell of the biplane fighter before the monoplane had proved itself, and had ordered the 240 mph (400 km/hr) Gladiator in 1935. Two monoplane fighters, the

Hurricane and the Spitfire, were the subjects of really substantial pre-war orders, but in September 1939 the RAF had in first-line service little more than three hundred Hurricanes and about half as many Spitfires – less than one-tenth of the totals then ordered. With a belated realisation of the RAF's weakness in the event of a war in Europe, a British Purchasing Mission went to the USA in 1938 to order substantial quantities of US combat aircraft to bridge the gap. However, these did not begin to become available in quantity until 1940; when war broke out in Europe Britain's fighter strength of Gladiators, Hurricanes and Spitfires was hugely outnumbered by that of the *Luftwaffe*.

In the initial advances through Poland, France and the Low Countries, the Nazi war machine met opposition which, although intrinsically valiant, was tactically and technically little better than that encountered by the German forces in Spain a year or two earlier. Dive-bombers and ground-attack aircraft, working in support of the ground troops, decimated much of the aerial opposition before it could get into the air, and such fighter opposition as did succeed in taking off was fairly easy prey for the *Luftwaffe*'s Bf 109 fighters.

After the rapid and successful advance to the Channel coast in 1939–40, the *Luftwaffe* began in the late spring of 1940 to step up its bombing campaign against the United Kingdom in preparation for the intended invasion of Britain. In Spain its medium bombers had been able to fly virtually unescorted and with only a light defensive armament, their performance being sufficient in itself to evade most of the fighters ranged against them. Such tactics were soon shown to be inadequate against the faster, well-armed Hurricanes and Spitfires, and twin-engined Messerschmitt Bf 110 long-range fighters were sent to escort the bombers. This revealed the first chink in the *Luftwaffe*'s armour, for the Bf 110 had never before been fully extended in the fighter role, and now proved unequal to its allotted task – so much so that single-engined Bf 109's had to be sent with the formations to escort the escorts.

On 18 June 1940 Winston Churchill told the House of Commons: 'What General Weygand called the Battle of France is over. I expect that the Battle of Britain is about to begin.' Britain's victory in that battle is rightly credited to 'the few', the men and machines that, greatly outnumbered, withstood the

Luftwaffe onslaught during September and October 1940. But 'the few' might have been a great deal fewer without the foresight of Air Chief Marshal Dowding, the C-in-C of RAF Fighter Command, who in May 1940 urged the government to resist the very natural temptation further to deplete its home defence squadrons by sending more and more fighters to support the hard-pressed Allied forces on the Continent.

The defeats inflicted upon its fighters in the Battle of Britain represented the first serious reversal the *Luftwaffe* had suffered during four militant years, and though the bomber *blitz* continued, with a measure of Italian support during the winter of 1940–41, some two thousand German aircraft were lost before the daylight attacks gave way to night bombing. During this phase of the war the Defiant turret-armed fighter, an unfortunate failure in daylight combat, salvaged something of its reputation by serving with some measure of success as a night fighter. The first truly effective night fighters of the war, however, were the twin-engined Beaufighter and Mosquito, both equipped with AI (airborne interception) radar and more effectively armed than the Defiant.

The *Luftwaffe*, attempting to recoup after its losses in 1940, had its efforts largely negated by Hitler's decision to invade the USSR in June 1941, thus creating an additional front along which its resources had to be dispersed. On the credit side, the Bf 109 now began to be joined in service by the superlative Focke-Wulf Fw 190; but when the invasion of Russia was followed less than six months later by the Japanese attack on Pearl Harbor, thus bringing the USA officially into the war, the Axis powers virtually sealed their own fate. The Soviet Union, whose aircraft had also figured in the fighting in Spain (and against the Japanese across the Siberian borders), was, like Britain, France, Poland and other European nations, still in the early stages of its latest modernisation programme at the time of the Nazi invasion. The Soviet Air Force was numerically strong, but its front-line aircraft were not modern by contemporary standards and, like the RAF, it was obliged to rely heavily at first upon large quantities of US warplanes supplied after the passing of the Lend-Lease Act in March 1941. Once it did begin, from 1942, to re-equip with domestically built aircraft it produced a number of combat types which, though of less refined design than the best Western types, were highly efficient weapons and were manufactured in prodigious quantities seldom matched before or since among military aircraft. These were mostly fighters or ground-attack designs, and among them was the archetype of nearly all subsequent ground-attack aircraft, the Ilyushin Il-2.

Pilots of the Japanese air forces shared with those of Italy a predilection for the open cockpit and the lightly armed but highly manoeuvrable fighter. The Japanese, however, had discarded the biplane formula somewhat earlier, all the principal first-line Army and Navy fighters being monoplanes. In the minds of most people, the Japanese fighters of the period are epitomised by the Mitsubishi Zero-Sen single-seater of the Japanese Naval Air Force, which outranked numerically and in renown any other Japanese type produced before 1945. The Zero was without doubt an excellent aeroplane, especially in the early stages of the war, although better fighters produced in smaller numbers included the Navy's Shiden-*Kai* and the Army's Ki-84 and Ki-100. Nor should Nakajima's elegant Hayabusa be omitted from the reckoning, for numerically it was the JAAF's most important fighter, and but for the lack of a more lethal armament would surely have made a greater impact. Japan's conduct of the war can be divided broadly into that on the mainland of south-east Asia, carried out chiefly by the Army Air Force, and that among the numerous island groups in the south-west Pacific, which was essentially the responsibility of the Naval Air Force. So long as it retained its aircraft carriers, the Japanese Fleet was a formidable adversary; but, as the war progressed and its carrier fleet was diminished and demolished, its power in the Pacific was reduced to negligible proportions. The Japanese Army overran the southern mainland of Asia so quickly at the outset of its offensive that its air force became very thinly spread over the vast area that it now had to cover, and eventually home production failed to keep pace with even the normal combat wastage of aircraft by each service.

When the USA entered the war on 7 December 1941, its aviation industry was already committed to the large orders placed in pre-war years by Britain, France and other countries, and to even greater output to meet the 1941 demands of Lend-Lease allocations to the Allies. Once the USA became committed as a combatant, this already huge work load on the domestic aircraft industry was increased still further by large production orders on behalf of its own forces and the acceptance for service of several newly developed combat types. At the outset, nearly one-third of the entire US productive effort was devoted to the manufacture of transport aircraft, and a high percentage of the remaining effort was concerned with the production of medium and heavy bombers and long-range patrol aircraft. It is a measure of the overall US output that, during the ensuing four years, more than 13,000 Warhawk, 20,000 Wildcat and Hellcat, 12,000 Corsair, 15,000 Thunderbolt and 12,000 Mustang fighters were turned out, in addition to lesser quantities of other fighters and miscellaneous other types.

In June 1942 Japan suffered a really serious defeat at US hands in the Battle of Midway Island, in the course of which Japan lost four aircraft carriers and over two hundred and fifty front-line aircraft. The Battle of Midway was a turning-point in the conduct of the Pacific war equal in importance to that of the Battle of Britain to the war in Europe. Within a year of Pearl Harbor, the number of aircraft in service with the US forces had trebled, and most of this strength was serving abroad. One of the first steps taken by the USAAF was the establishment of the US Eighth Air Force at bases in the United Kingdom, and in the autumn of 1942 part of the Eighth was detached to form the basis of the US Twelfth Air Force in North Africa.

In 1943, after the successful conclusion of the North African campaign, first Sicily and then Italy were invaded. By this time Britain's Fleet Air Arm was at last beginning to receive more modern monoplane fighters of British design, to replace its antiquated Sea Gladiator biplanes and augment the American monoplane types received earlier under Lend-Lease. One effect of the mounting bombing campaign against Germany was the wholesale recall of *Luftwaffe* fighter squadrons from other fronts, from which they could ill be spared, to defend the German homeland; moreover, defensive fighters were now outnumbering bombers in the overall *Luftwaffe* establishment, and it was Germany's turn to introduce specialist night fighters into service. Nevertheless, by cutting its reserves to negligible proportions, the *Luftwaffe* was still able to claim a first-line strength in mid-1943 of around four thousand aircraft.

On 8 September 1943 the Italian forces under the command

of Marshal Badoglio surrendered to the Allies, and the aircraft based in Italy became divided into two opposing camps. Those in that half of Italy which had still not been reached by the Allied advance were formed into the *Aviazione della Repubblica Sociale Italiana* and continued to fight alongside the *Luftwaffe*, while those in southern Italy became known as the Italian Co-Belligerent Air Force, which continued to operate with a mixture of Italian, American and British aircraft in support of the Allied cause. Toward the end of 1943 the forthcoming invasion of the Continent was foreshadowed by the setting up in November of the Allied Second Tactical Air Force, and by the increase in ground-attack raids against enemy targets in Europe.

On 6 June 1944 the long-awaited invasion of Normandy began, and was supported strongly by hard-won air superiority and by continual low-level harassing of enemy ground forces by fighter-type aircraft armed with bombs, cannon and rocket projectiles, as well as by sustained heavy bombing attacks on German-held industrial targets. Evidence of desperation in the face of impending defeat manifested itself in both hemispheres during the second half of 1944. In Europe it took the form of Hitler's *Vergeltungs-waffen* (Reprisal Weapons), the V1 and the V2. The V1 flying bombs constituted a slight setback for a time in the autumn of 1944, but their measure was soon taken by the piston-engined Mustangs and Thunderbolts of the USAAF and the Tempests of the RAF, and the latter service's jet-engined Meteor fighters. Repeated attacks on their factories and launching sites finally disposed of the menace both from the V1 and from the V2 rocket missiles which were used against Britain for a time during 1944–45. The hard-hit German aviation industry achieved a partial respite by an extensive dispersal of its factories and by setting up new plants underground, almost exclusively by this time for the production of defensive fighters; but even these new aircraft were prevented from entering service in the numbers needed, due to the continued attentions of Allied bombers to their factories and airfields.

The methods adopted by the Japanese air forces in the latter part of 1944 took an even more extreme form: that of the suicide attack. These attacks, carried out by both Army and Navy pilots, were made for the most part in standard service aircraft of all kinds, carrying bombs or internally stowed explosive; their pilots simply flew them straight into their target and perished in the resulting explosion. Such tactics inevitably had at least an initial effect upon the morale of Allied troops, and so far as results were concerned were quite effective for a time. Incomprehensible as this form of warfare may have been to non-Oriental minds, it was responsible in ten months for more than forty-eight per cent of all American warships damaged, and over twenty-one per cent of those sunk, during the entire course of the war: small wonder that an official survey later rated it 'the single most effective weapon developed by the Japanese in World War 2'. The literally suicidal resistance of the Japanese reached a fantastic peak in the battles for Iwo Jima and Okinawa. In the twelve weeks' battle for Okinawa even the heavy casualties in US troops and weapons paled into insignificance beside the Japanese losses of one hundred and seventeen thousand personnel and three thousand eight hundred aircraft. By this time, however, the USAAF had begun, from bases in the Marianas Islands regained for it by the US Navy, to carry out a sustained bombing of targets within Japan with its long-range, high-flying B-29 Superfortresses; and although Japanese suicide attacks were by no means discontinued, their ferocity and their effect diminished steadily after Okinawa.

In Europe in 1945, neither the advent of the Me 262 and Me 163 jet- and rocket-powered fighters nor the launching of V2 rockets against Britain seriously affected the final outcome of the war, and the *Luftwaffe*, already deprived by Allied bombing of the new fighters it desperately needed, was driven to the final indignity of having its surviving aircraft virtually all grounded for lack of fuel; while the Japanese air forces, driven back to defend their homeland against the American bombers, had all their efforts negated when the atomic *coups de grâce* were delivered upon Hiroshima and Nagasaki in August 1945.

THE COLOUR PLATES

As an aid to identification, the eighty colour plates which follow have been arranged in an essentially visual order, within the broad sequence: biplanes, single-engined monoplanes and multi-engined monoplanes. The sole rocket-powered aircraft appears last of all. The reference number of each type corresponds to the appropriate text matter, and an index to all types illustrated appears on pp. 162–163.

The 'split' plan view, adopted to give both upper and lower surface markings within a single plan outline, depicts the colour scheme appearing above and below either the port half or starboard half of the aircraft, according to whichever aspect is shown in the side elevation. This should be borne in mind when studying, for example, the plan views of US aircraft in which, normally, the national insignia appear only on the port upper and starboard lower surfaces of the wings.

1

De Havilland Tiger Moth II of the R.A.F. (unit unidentified), *ca.* autumn 1940.
Engine: One 130 h.p. de Havilland Gipsy Major 1 inverted-Vee type. *Span:*
29 ft. 4 in. (8·94 m.). *Length:* 23 ft. 11 in. (7·34 m.). *Height:* 8 ft. 9½ in. (2·68 m.).
Normal take-off weight: 1,825 lb. (828 kg.). *Maximum speed:* 109 m.p.h.
(175 km./hr.) at 1,000 ft. (305 m.). *Operational ceiling:* 13,600 ft. (4,145 m.).
Range: 302 miles (486 km.). *Armament:* None.

KAYDET (U.S.A.)

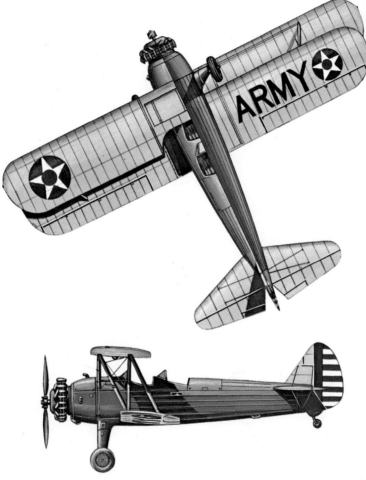

2

Boeing- Stearman PT-13D Kaydet of the U.S.A.A.F., 1942. *Engine:* One 220 h.p. Lycoming R-680-17 radial. *Span:* 32 ft. 2 in. (9·80 m.). *Length:* 25 ft. 0¼ in. (7·63 m.). *Height:* 9 ft. 2 in. (2·79 m.). *Normal take-off weight:* 2,717 lb. (1,232 kg.). *Maximum speed:* 124 m.p.h. (200 km./hr.) at sea level. *Operational ceiling:* 11,400 ft. (3,475 m.). *Normal range:* 505 miles (813 km.). *Armament:* None.

HENSCHEL Hs 123 (Germany)

3

Henschel Hs 123A-1 of 8/SG.1, Eastern Front, spring 1942. *Engine:* One 880 h.p.
BMW 132Dc radial. *Span:* 34 ft. 5⅜ in. (10·50 m.). *Length:* 27 ft. 4 in. (8·33 m.).
Height: 10 ft. 6⅜ in. (3·21 m.). *Normal take-off weight:* 4,894 lb. (2,220 kg.).
Maximum speed: 211 m.p.h. (340 km./hr.) at 3,940 ft. (1,200 m.). *Operational
ceiling:* 29,530 ft. (9,000 m.). *Maximum range:* 534 miles (860 km.). *Armament:*
Two 7·9 mm. MG 17 machine-guns in upper engine cowling; provision for two
20 mm. MG FF cannon, four 110 lb. (50 kg.) bombs or canisters of smaller
bombs beneath lower wings.

FIAT C.R.42 (Italy)

4

Fiat C.R.42 (J 11) of the 2nd Air Division, F 9 Wing Royal Swedish Air Force, *ca.* 1941. *Engine:* One 840 h.p. Fiat A.74R.1C 38 radial. *Span:* 31 ft. 9$\frac{7}{8}$ in. (9·70 m.). *Length:* 27 ft. 1$\frac{1}{8}$ in. (8·26 m.). *Height:* 11 ft. 9$\frac{1}{8}$ in. (3·585 m.). *Normal take-off weight:* 5,033 lb. (2,283 kg.). *Maximum speed:* 267 m.p.h. (430 km./hr.) at 17,490 ft. (5,330 m.). *Operational ceiling:* 33,465 ft. (10,200 m.). *Normal range:* 482 miles (775 km.). *Armament:* Two 12·7 mm. Breda-SAFAT machine-guns in upper front fuselage; provision for two similar guns or two 220 lb. (100 kg.) bombs beneath lower wings.

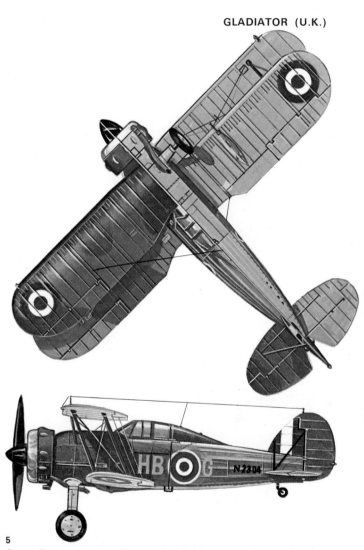

5

Gloster Gladiator II of No. 239 Squadron R.A.F., autumn 1940. *Engine:* One 725 h.p. Bristol Mercury VIIIA radial. *Span:* 32 ft. 3 in. (9·83 m.). *Length:* 27 ft. 5 in. (8·36 m.). *Height:* 10 ft. 7 in. (3·23 m.). *Normal take-off weight:* 4,864 lb. (2,206 kg.). *Maximum speed:* 257 m.p.h. (414 km./hr.) at 14,600 ft. (4,450 m.). *Operational ceiling:* 33,500 ft. (10,211 m.). *Normal range:* 444 miles (715 km.). *Armament:* Two 0·303 in. Browning machine-guns on sides of front fuselage, and one beneath each lower wing.

PZL P.11c (Poland)

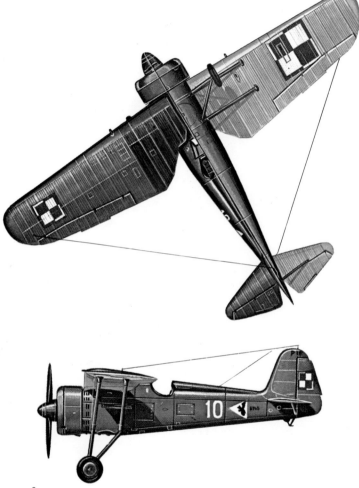

6

PZL P.11c of No. 113 (Owl) Squadron, 1st Air Regiment Polish Air Force, Warsaw, September 1939. *Engine:* One 560 h.p. PZL Skoda-built Bristol Mercury V S2 radial. *Span:* 35 ft. 2 in. (10·72 m.). *Length:* 24 ft. 9¼ in. (7·55 m.). *Height:* 9 ft. 4¼ in. (2·85 m.). *Maximum take-off weight:* 3,505 lb. (1,590 kg.). *Maximum speed:* 230 m.p.h. (370 km./hr.) at 14,760 ft. (4,500 m.). *Operational ceiling:* 31,170 ft. (9,500 m.). *Normal range:* 503 miles (810 km.). *Armament:* Two 0·303 in. Vickers or 7·7 mm. Wzor 37 machine-guns in fuselage sides and (on some aircraft) one in each wing; provision for two 27·5 lb. (12·5 kg.) bombs beneath each wing.

7

Chance Vought F4U-1A Corsair of Squadron VF-17 U.S. Navy, summer 1943. *Engine:* One 2,000 h.p. Pratt & Whitney R-2800-8 Double Wasp radial. *Span:* 40 ft. 11¾ in. (12·49 m.). *Length:* 33 ft. 4½ in. (10·17 m.). *Height:* 14 ft. 9¼ in. (4·50 m.). *Normal take-off weight:* 11,093 lb. (5,032 kg.). *Maximum speed:* 417 m.p.h. (671 km./hr.) at 19,900 ft. (6,065 m.). *Operational ceiling:* 36,900 ft. (11,247 m.). *Normal range:* 1,015 miles (1,633 km.). *Armament:* Three 0·50 in. Browning machine-guns in each wing.

WILDCAT (U.S.A.)

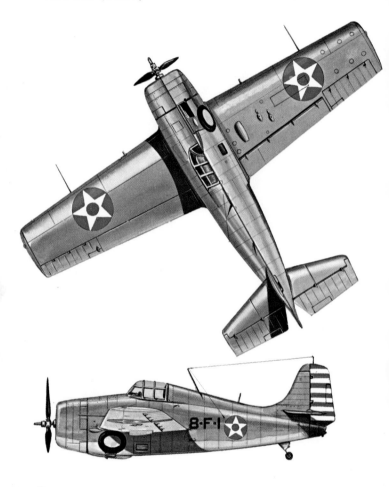

8

Grumman F4F-3 Wildcat of Squadron VF-8, U.S.S. *Hornet*, late 1941. *Engine:*
One 1,200 h.p. Pratt & Whitney R-1830-76 Twin Wasp radial. *Span:* 38 ft. 0 in.
(11·58 m.). *Length:* 28 ft. 9 in. (8·76 m.). *Height:* 9 ft. 2½ in. (2·81 m.). *Normal
take-off weight:* 7,002 lb. (3,176 kg.). *Maximum speed:* 330 m.p.h. (531 km./hr.)
at 21,100 ft. (6,431 m.). *Operational ceiling:* 37,500 ft. (11,430 m.). *Normal
range:* 845 miles (1,360 km.). *Armament:* Two 0·50 in. M-2 Browning machine-
guns in each wing; provision for one 100 lb. (45·4 kg.) bomb beneath each wing.

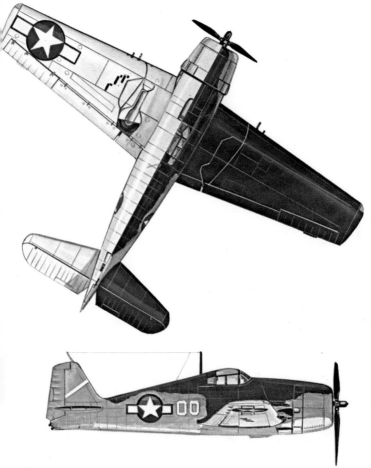

9

Grumman F6F-3 Hellcat of Squadron VF-9, U.S.S. *Yorktown*, September 1943. *Engine:* One 2,000 h.p. Pratt & Whitney R-2800-10 Double Wasp radial. *Span:* 42 ft. 10 in. (13·06 m.). *Length:* 33 ft. 7 in. (10·24 m.). *Height:* 14 ft. 5 in. (4·39 m.). *Normal take-off weight:* 12,441 lb. (5,643 kg.). *Maximum speed:* 375 m.p.h. (604 km./hr.) at 17,300 ft. (5,273 m.). *Operational ceiling:* 37,300 ft. (11,369 m.). *Normal range:* 1,090 miles (1,754 km.). *Armament:* Three 0·50 in. Browning M-2 machine-guns in each wing.

THUNDERBOLT (U.S.A.)

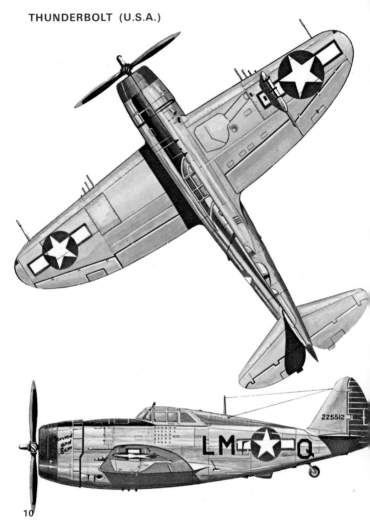

10

Republic P-47D-21-RE of the 61st Fighter Squadron, 56th Fighter Group U.S.A.A.F., U.K. May 1944. *Engine:* One 2,300 h.p. Pratt & Whitney R-2800-21 Double Wasp radial. *Span:* 40 ft. 9¾ in. (12·43 m.). *Length:* 36 ft. 1¾ in. (11·02 m.). *Height:* 14 ft. 7 in. (4·45 m.). *Normal take-off weight:* 13,500 lb. (5,920 kg.). *Maximum speed:* 433 m.p.h. (697 km./hr.) at 30,000 ft. (9,144 m.). *Operational ceiling:* 40,000 ft. (12,192 m.). *Normal range:* 640 miles (1,030 km.). *Armament:* Four 0·50 in. Browning M-2 machine-guns in each wing; provision for one 500 lb. (227 kg.) bomb beneath fuselage and one similar bomb or an auxiliary fuel tank beneath each wing.

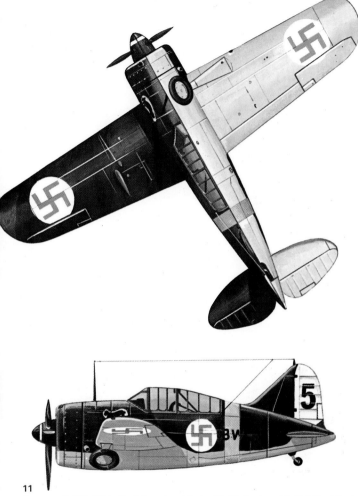

11

Brewster B-239 (F2A-1) of Squadron HLeLv 24, Air Regiment LeR 2 Finnish Air Force, 1941–42. *Engine:* One 940 h.p. Wright R-1820-34 Cyclone radial. *Span:* 35 ft. 0 in. (10·67 m.). *Length:* 26 ft. 4 in. (8·03 m.). *Height:* 12 ft. 1 in. (3·68 m.). *Normal take-off weight:* 5,055 lb. (2,293 kg.). *Maximum speed:* 301 m.p.h. (484 km./hr.) at 17,000 ft. (5,182 m.). *Operational ceiling:* 32,500 ft. (9,906 m.). *Normal range:* 1,095 miles (1,762 km.). *Armament:* Two 0·50 in. Colt-Browning machine-guns in upper engine cowling and one in each wing.

NAKAJIMA Ki-27 (Japan)

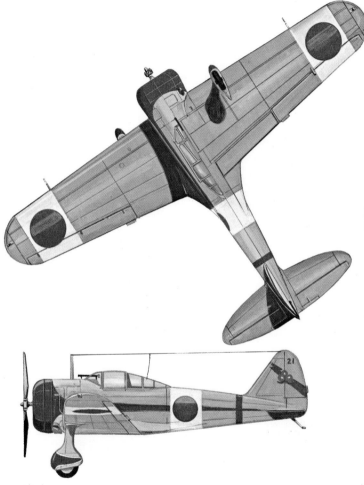

12

Nakajima Ki-27b of the 2nd Squadron, 246th Group J.A.A.F., home defence of Japan, 1942–43. *Engine:* One 710 h.p. Nakajima Ha.1b radial. *Span:* 37 ft. 0⅞ in. (11·30 m.). *Length:* 24 ft. 8½ in. (7·53 m.). *Height:* 10 ft. 8 in. (3·25 m.). *Normal take-off weight:* 3,638 lb. (1,650 kg.). *Maximum speed:* 286 m.p.h. (460 km./hr.) at 11,485 ft. (3,500 m.). *Normal range:* 388 miles (625 km.). *Armament:* Two 7·7 mm. Type 89 machine-guns in front fuselage; provision for two 55 lb. (25 kg.) bombs beneath each wing.

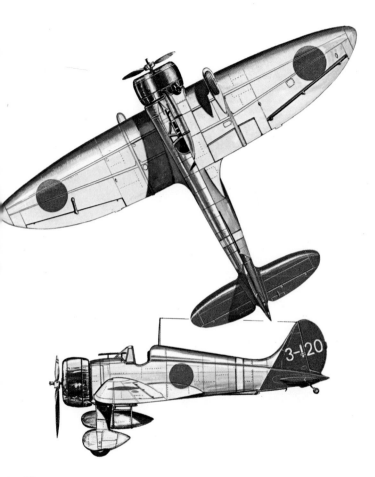

13

Mitsubishi A5M4 Model 24, believed to be an aircraft of No. 12 Air Corps J.N.A.F., late 1939. *Engine:* One 710 h.p. Nakajima Kotobuki 41 radial. *Span:* 36 ft. 1⅛ in. (11·00 m.). *Length:* 24 ft. 9⅞ in. (7·565 m.). *Height:* 10 ft. 6 in. (3·20 m.). *Normal take-off weight:* 3,684 lb. (1,671 kg.). *Maximum speed:* 270 m.p.h. (435 km./hr.) at 9,845 ft. (3,000 m.). *Operational ceiling:* 32,150 ft. (9,800 m.). *Range with auxiliary fuel tank:* 746 miles (1,200 km.). *Armament:* Two 7·7 mm. Type 89 machine-guns in upper front fuselage; provision for two 66 lb. (30 kg.) bombs.

VALIANT (U.S.A.)

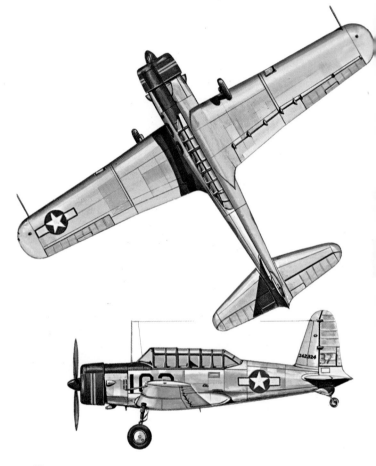

14

Vultee BT-13A Valiant of the U.S.A.A.F., summer 1943. *Engine:* One 450 h.p. Pratt & Whitney R-985-AN-1 Wasp Junior radial. *Span:* 42 ft. 0 in. (12·80 m.). *Length:* 29 ft. 2 in. (8·89 m.). *Height:* 11 ft. 6 in. (3·51 m.). *Normal take-off weight:* 3,991 lb. (1,810 kg.). *Maximum speed:* 182 m.p.h. (293 km./hr.) at sea level. *Operational ceiling:* 21,000 ft. (6,401 m.). *Normal range:* 725 miles (1,167 km.). *Armament:* None.

15

Blackburn Roc of No. 801 Squadron Fleet Air Arm, *ca.* June 1940. *Engine:* One
905 h.p. Bristol Perseus XII radial. *Span:* 46 ft. 0 in. (14·02 m.). *Length:* 35 ft. 7 in.
(10·85 m.). *Height:* 12 ft. 1 in. (3·68 m.). *Normal take-off weight:* 8,800 lb.
(3,992 kg.). *Maximum speed:* 196 m.p.h. (315 km./hr.) at 6,500 ft. (1,981 m.).
Operational ceiling: 15,200 ft. (4,633 m.). *Normal range:* 610 miles (982 km.).
Armament: Four 0·303 in. Browning machine-guns in dorsal turret; provision
for four 30 lb. (13·6 kg.) bombs beneath each wing.

BOOMERANG (Australia)

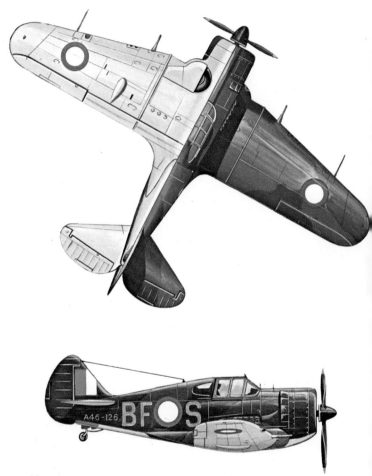

16

Commonwealth CA-13 Boomerang of No. 5 Squadron R.A.A.F., Mareeba (Queensland) March 1944. *Engine:* One 1,200 h.p. CAC-built Pratt & Whitney R-1830-S3C4-G Twin Wasp radial. *Span:* 36 ft. 0 in. (10·97 m.). *Length:* 26 ft. 9 in. (8·15 m.). *Height:* 13 ft. 0 in. (3·96 m.). *Normal take-off weight:* 7,699 lb. (3,492 kg.). *Maximum speed:* 305 m.p.h. (491 km./hr.) at 15,500 ft. (4,724 m.). *Operational ceiling:* 34,000 ft. (10,363 m.). *Normal range:* 930 miles (1,497 km.). *Armament:* One 20 mm Hispano cannon and two 0·303 in. Browning machine-guns in each wing.

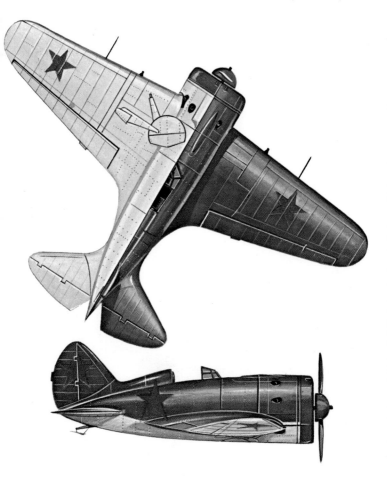

17

Polikarpov I-16 Type 24 of the VVS (Soviet Air Force), 1941. *Engine:* One 1,000 h.p. Shvetsov M-62 radial. *Span:* 29 ft. 6⅜ in. (9·00 m.). *Length:* 20 ft. 1⅛ in. (6·125 m.). *Height:* 8 ft. 5 in. (2·565 m.). *Maximum take-off weight:* 4,519 lb. (2,050 kg.). *Maximum speed:* 326 m.p.h. (525 km./hr.) at 14,765 ft. (4,500 m.). *Operational ceiling:* 29,530 ft. (9,000 m.). *Normal range:* 249 miles (400 km.). *Armament:* Two 7·62 mm. ShKAS machine-guns in upper front fuselage and one 20 mm. ShVAK cannon in each wing; provision for up to three 82 mm. RS-82 rocket projectiles beneath each wing.

MACCHI C.200 (Italy)

18

Macchi C.200 *Saetta* of the 372° *Squadriglia*, 152° *Gruppo*, 54° *Stormo*, Cyrenaica autumn 1941. *Engine:* One 870 h.p. Fiat A.74 RC 38 radial. *Span:* 34 ft. 8½ in. (10·58 m.). *Length:* 26 ft. 10⅝ in. (8·196 m.). *Height:* 11 ft. 6¼ in. (3·51 m.). *Normal take-off weight:* 5,132 lb. (2,328 kg.). *Maximum speed:* 313 m.p.h. (503 km./hr.) at 14,765 ft. (4,500 m.). *Operational ceiling:* 29,200 ft. (8,900 m.). *Range:* 354 miles (570 km.). *Armament:* Two 12·7 mm. Breda-SAFAT machine-guns in upper front fuselage; provision for one 110, 220 or 353 lb. (50, 100 or 160 kg.) bomb beneath each wing.

FIAT G.50 (Italy)

19

Fiat G.50*bis* of the 151° *Squadriglia*, 20° *Gruppo*, 51° *Stormo*, Libya *ca.*
November 1941. *Engine:* One 870 h.p. Fiat A.74 RC 38 radial. *Span:* 36 ft. 1⅛ in.
(11·00 m.). *Length:* 27 ft. 2⅜ in. (8·29 m.). *Height:* approx. 11 ft. 9¾ in. (3·60 m.).
Normal take-off weight: 5,512 lb. (2,500 kg.). *Maximum speed:* 302 m.p.h.
(486 km./hr.) at 19,685 ft. (6,000 m.). *Operational ceiling:* 35,270 ft.
(10,750 m.). *Normal range:* 294 miles (473 km.). *Armament:* Two 12·7 mm.
Breda-SAFAT machine-guns in upper front fuselage.

FFVS J 22 (Sweden)

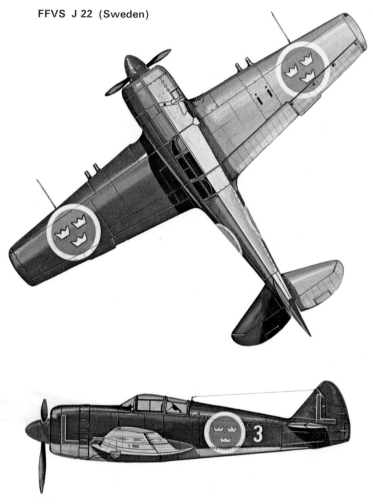

20

FFVS J 22B of the 1st Air Division, F 3 Wing Royal Swedish Air Force, 1945. *Engine:* One 1,200 h.p. SFA-built Pratt & Whitney R-1830-S1C3-G Twin Wasp radial. *Span:* 32 ft. $9\frac{3}{4}$ in. (10·00 m.). *Length:* 25 ft. $7\frac{1}{8}$ in. (7·80 m.). *Height:* 9 ft. $2\frac{1}{4}$ in. (2·80 m.). *Normal take-off weight:* 6,250 lb. (2,835 kg.). *Maximum speed:* 357 m.p.h. (575 km./hr.) at 11,485 ft. (3,500 m.). *Operational ceiling:* 30,510 ft. (9,300 m.). *Maximum range:* 789 miles (1,270 km.). *Armament:* Two 13·2 mm. M/39A machine-guns in each wing.

21

Focke-Wulf Fw 190A-4 of 9/JG.2 *Richthofen*, Vannes (France) February 1943.
Engine: One 1,700 h.p. BMW 801D-2 radial (2,100 h.p. at altitude with MW 50
boost). *Span:* 34 ft. 5⅜ in. (10·50 m.). *Length:* 28 ft. 10½ in. (8·80 m.). *Height:*
13 ft. 0 in. (3·96 m.). *Normal take-off weight:* 8,378 lb. (3,800 kg.). *Maximum
speed:* 416 m.p.h. (670 km./hr.) at 20,590 ft. (6,275 m.). *Operational ceiling:*
37,400 ft. (11,400 m.). *Normal range:* 497 miles (800 km.). *Armament:* Two
7·9 mm. MG 17 machine-guns in upper front fuselage, and one 20 mm. MG 151
and one 20 mm. MG FF cannon in each wing.

MYRSKY (Finland)

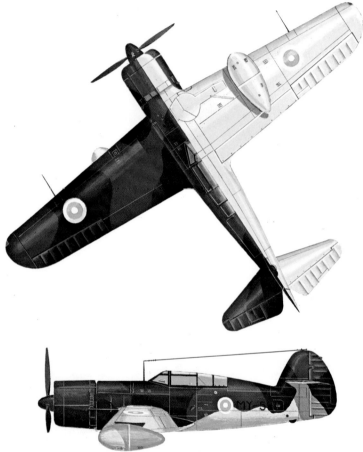

22

IVL Myrsky II of the Finnish Air Force, winter 1944–45. *Engine:* One 1,065 h.p. SFA-built Pratt & Whitney R-1830-S1C3-G Twin Wasp radial. *Span:* 36 ft. 1⅛ in. (11·00 m.). *Length:* 27 ft. 4¾ in. (8·35 m.). *Height:* 9 ft. 10⅜ in. (3·00 m.). *Normal take-off weight:* 6,504 lb. (2,950 kg.). *Maximum speed:* 329 m.p.h. (530 km./hr.) at 10,665 ft. (3,250 m.). *Operational ceiling:* 29,530 ft. (9,000 m.). *Normal range:* 311 miles (500 km.). *Armament:* Four 12·7 mm. Browning machine-guns in upper front fuselage.

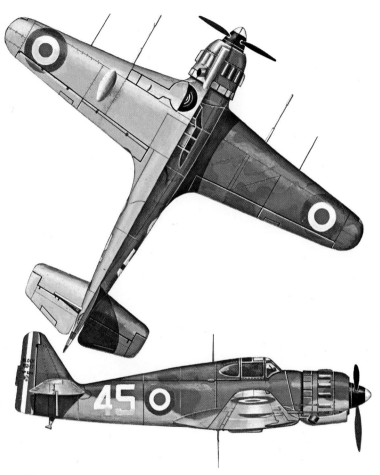

23

Bloch 152-C1 of GC.II/9, *Armée de l'Air*, Clermont Ferrand, June 1940. *Engine:* One 1,060 h.p. Gnome-Rhône 14N-49 radial. *Span:* 34 ft. 7 in. (10·542 m.). *Length:* 29 ft. 10⅜ in. (9·104 m.). *Height:* 9 ft. 11¼ in. (3·03 m.). *Normal take-off weight:* 6,058 lb. (2,748 kg.). *Maximum speed:* 316 m.p.h. (509 km./hr.) at 13,125 ft. (4,000 m.). *Operational ceiling:* 32,810 ft. (10,000 m.). *Normal range:* 336 miles (540 km.). *Armament:* One 20 mm. Hispano HS 404 cannon and one 7·5 mm. MAC 1934-M39 machine-gun in each wing.

FOKKER D.XXI (Netherlands)

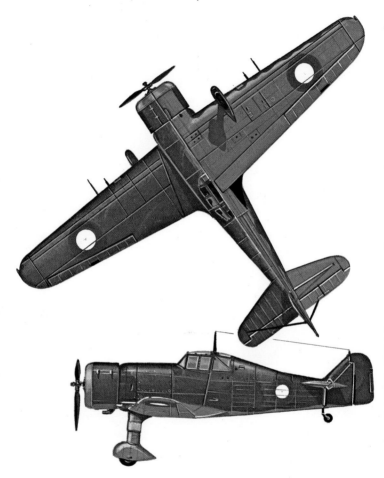

24

Danish-built Fokker D.XXI of No. 2 *Eskadrille*, Royal Danish Aviation Troops, Værløse, early 1940. *Engine:* One 760 h.p. Bristol Mercury VIII radial. *Span:* 36 ft. 1⅛ in. (11·00 m.). *Length:* 26 ft. 11¼ in. (8·21 m.). *Height:* 9 ft. 8⅛ in. (2·95 m.). *Normal take-off weight:* 4,519 lb. (2,050 kg.). *Maximum speed:* 286 m.p.h. (460 km./hr.) at 16,730 ft. (5,100 m.). *Operational ceiling:* 36,090 ft. (11,000 m.). *Normal range:* 528 miles (850 km.). *Armament:* One 8 mm. DISA machine-gun in each wing; provision for four 27·5 lb. (12·5 kg.) bombs beneath each wing.

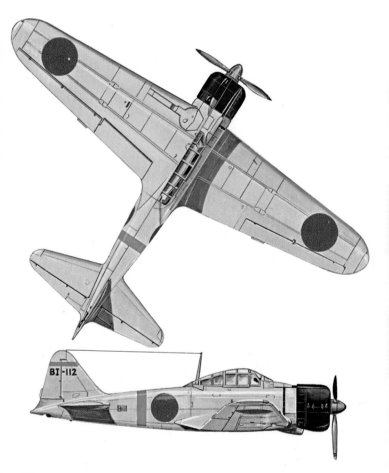

25
Mitsubishi A6M2 Model 21 *Zero-Sen* from the carrier *Soryu*, engaged in the attack on Port Darwin, February 1942. *Engine:* One 940 h.p. Nakajima Sakae 12 radial. *Span:* 39 ft. 4½ in. (12·00 m.). *Length:* 29 ft. 8¾ in. (9·06 m.). *Height:* 10 ft. 0⅛ in. (3·05 m.). *Normal take-off weight:* 5,313 lb. (2,410 kg.). *Maximum speed:* 332 m.p.h. (535 km./hr.) at 14,930 ft. (4,550 m.). *Operational ceiling:* 32,810 ft. (10,000 m.). *Normal range:* 1,162 miles (1,870 km.). *Armament:* Two 7·7 mm. Type 97 machine-guns in upper front fuselage and one 20 mm. Type 99 cannon in each wing; provision for one 132 lb. (60 kg.) bomb beneath each wing.

REGGIANE Re 2000 (Italy)

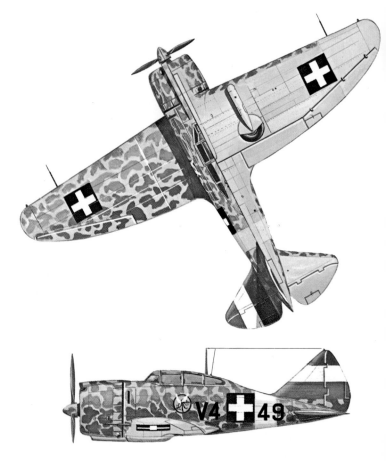

26

Reggiane Re 2000 *Serie* I of No. 1/1 Fighter Squadron Hungarian Independent Fighter Group, Eastern Front summer 1942. *Engine:* One 986 h.p. Piaggio P.XI RC 40 radial. *Span:* 36 ft. 1⅛ in. (11·00 m.). *Length:* 26 ft. 2½ in. (7·99 m.). *Height:* 10 ft. 6 in. (3·20 m.). *Normal take-off weight:* 6,349 lb. (2,880 kg.). *Maximum speed:* 329 m.p.h. (530 km./hr.) at 16,405 ft. (5,000 m.). *Operational ceiling:* 31,170 ft. (9,500 m.). *Normal range:* 715 miles (1,150 km.). *Armament:* Two 12·7 mm. Breda-SAFAT machine-guns in upper engine cowling.

27

Lavochkin La-5FN of the VVS (Soviet Air Force), Eastern Front 1944. *Engine:* One 1,650 h.p. Shvetsov M-82FN radial. *Span:* 32 ft. 1⅞ in. (9·80 m.). *Length:* 27 ft. 10⅝ in. (8·50 m.). *Height:* 8 ft. 4 in. (2·54 m.). *Normal take-off weight:* 7,408 lb. (3,360 kg.). *Maximum speed:* 402 m.p.h. (647 km./hr.) at 16,405 ft. (5,000 m.). *Operational ceiling:* 32,810 ft. (10,000 m.). *Range:* 435 miles (700 km.). *Armament:* Two 20 mm. ShVAK or 23 mm. NS cannon in upper engine cowling; provision for two 82 mm. RS-82 rocket projectiles or 331 lb. (150 kg.) bombs beneath each wing.

NAKAJIMA Ki-43 (Japan)

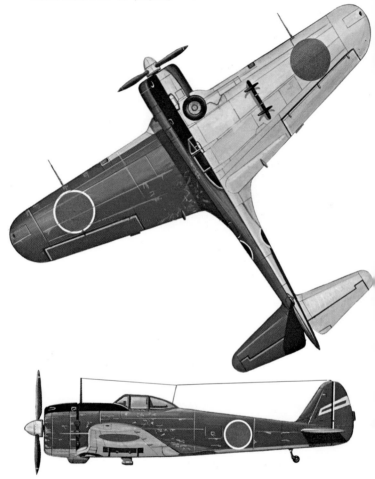

28

Nakajima Ki-43-IIIa Model 3A *Hayabusa* of the 20th Group J.A.A.F., home defence of Japan 1944–45. *Engine:* One 1,190 h.p. Mitsubishi Ha-112 radial. *Span:* 35 ft. 6¾ in. (10·84 m.). *Length:* 29 ft. 3⅛ in. (8·92 m.). *Height:* 10 ft. 8¾ in. (3·27 m.). *Maximum take-off weight:* 6,746 lb. (3,060 kg.). *Maximum speed:* 342 m.p.h. (550 km./hr.) at 19,195 ft. (5,850 m.). *Operational ceiling:* 37,400 ft. (11,400 m.). *Maximum range:* 1,988 miles (3,200 km.). *Armament:* Two 12·7 mm. Type 1 machine-guns in upper engine cowling; provision for one 110 lb. (50 kg.) or 220 lb. (100 kg.) bomb beneath each wing.

NAKAJIMA Ki-44 (Japan)

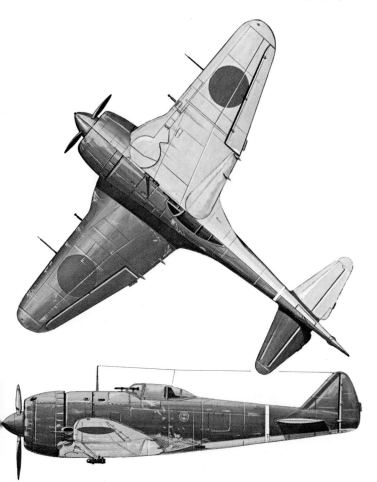

29

Eighth prototype Nakajima Ki-44-I *Shoki,* of the 3rd Flight, 47th Direct Command Squadron J.A.A.F., French Indochina January 1942. *Engine:* One 1,200 h.p. Nakajima Ha-41 radial. *Span:* 31 ft. 0 in. (9·45 m.). *Length:* 28 ft. 8½ in. (8·75 m.). *Height:* 10 ft. 8 in. (3·25 m.). *Normal take-off weight:* 5,512 lb. (2,500 kg.). *Maximum speed:* 360 m.p.h. (580 km./hr.) at 12,140 ft. (3,700 m.). *Operational ceiling:* 35,500 ft. (10,820 m.). *Normal range:* 575 miles (926 km.). *Armament:* Two 7·7 mm. Type 89 machine-guns in upper engine cowling and one 12·7 mm. Type 1 machine-gun in each wing.

NAKAJIMA Ki-84 (Japan)

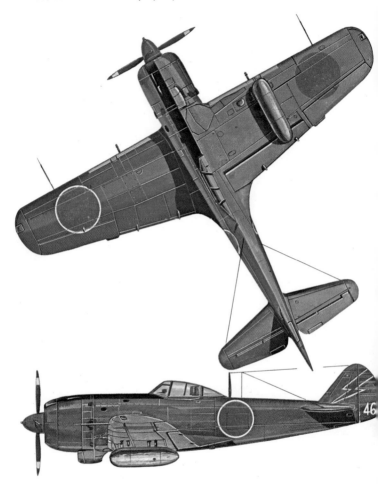

30

Nakajima Ki-84-Ia Model 1A *Hayate* of the 2nd Squadron, 11th Group J.A.A.F., Leyte Island (Philippines) late autumn 1944. *Engine:* One 1,990 h.p. Nakajima Ha-45-21 radial. *Span:* 36 ft. 10⅛ in. (11·238 m.). *Length:* 32 ft. 6½ in. (9·92 m.). *Height:* 11 ft. 1¼ in. (3·385 m.). *Normal take-off weight:* 7,940 lb. (3,602 kg.). *Maximum speed:* 427 m.p.h. (687 km./hr.) at 20,000 ft. (6,096 m.). *Operational ceiling:* 38,000 ft. (11,582 m.). *Normal range:* 780 miles (1,255 km.). *Armament:* Two 12·7 mm. Type 103 machine-guns in upper front fuselage and one 20 mm. Type 5 cannon in each wing; provision for one bomb of up to 551 lb. (250 kg.) size beneath each wing.

MITSUBISHI J2M (Japan)

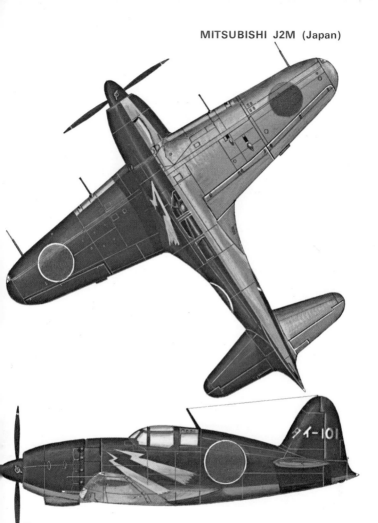

31

Mitsubishi J2M3 Model 21 *Raiden* of the Tainan Air Corps, J.N.A.F., 1943–44.
Engine: One 1,820 h.p. Mitsubishi Kasei 23a radial. *Span:* 35 ft. 5¼ in. (10·80 m.).
Length: 31 ft. 9¾ in. (9·695 m.). *Height:* 12 ft. 6 in. (3·81 m.). *Normal take-off
weight:* 7,573 lb. (3,435 kg.). *Maximum speed:* 380 m.p.h. (612 km./hr.) at
19,685 ft. (6,000 m.). *Operational ceiling:* 37,795 ft. (11,520 m.). *Normal range:*
656 miles (1,055 km.). *Armament:* One 20 mm. Type 99-I and one Type 99-II
cannon in each wing; provision for one 66 lb. (30 kg.) or 132 lb. (60 kg.) bomb
beneath each wing.

KAWANISHI N1K (Japan)

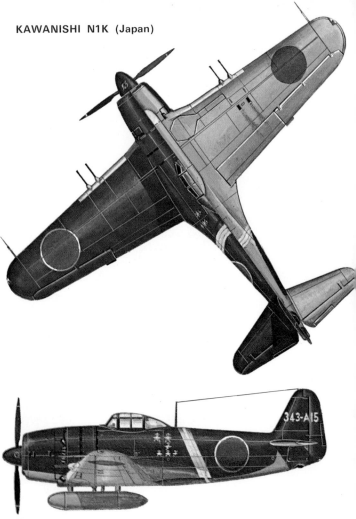

32

Kawanishi N1K2-J Model 21 *Shiden-Kai* of the 343rd Air Corps, J.N.A.F., 1944–45. *Engine:* One 1,990 h.p. Nakajima Homare 21 radial. *Span:* 39 ft. 3¼ in. (11·97 m.). *Length:* 30 ft. 8⅛ in. (9·35 m.). *Height:* 13 ft. 0 in. (3·96 m.). *Normal take-off weight:* 8,818 lb. (4,000 kg.). *Maximum speed:* 369 m.p.h. (594 km./hr.) at 18,375 ft. (5,600 m.). *Operational ceiling:* 35,300 ft. (10,760 m.). *Normal range:* 1,069 miles (1,720 km.). *Armament:* Two 20 mm. Type 99-II cannon in each wing; provision for one 551 lb. (250 kg.) bomb beneath each wing.

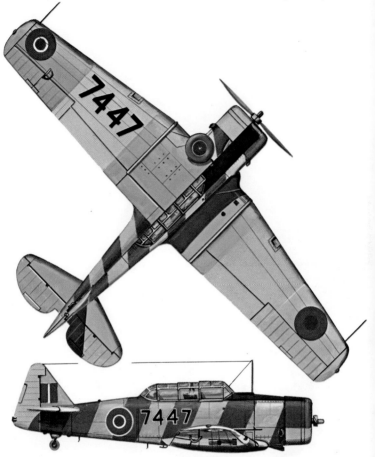

33

North American Harvard III (AT-6D) of No. 22 Air School, Southern Rhodesia
Air Force, Vereeniging (Southern Rhodesia), 1944. *Engine:* One 600 h.p.
Pratt & Whitney R-1340-AN-1 Wasp radial. *Span:* 42 ft. $0\frac{1}{4}$ in. (12·81 m.).
Length: 28 ft. $11\frac{7}{8}$ in. (8·84 m.). *Height:* 11 ft. $8\frac{1}{2}$ in. (3·57 m.). *Normal take-off
weight:* 5,300 lb. (2,404 kg.). *Maximum speed:* 208 m.p.h. (335 km./hr.) at
5,000 ft. (1,524 m.). *Operational ceiling:* 24,200 ft. (7,376 m.). *Normal range:*
730 miles (1,175 km.). *Armament:* Provision for one 0·30 in. machine-gun in
upper front fuselage and one in rear cockpit.

MARTINET (U.K.)

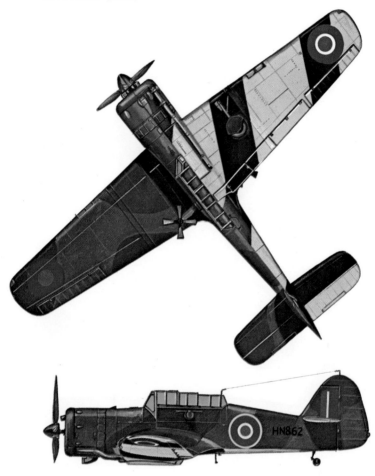

34

Miles Martinet TT I of the R.A.F. (unit unidentified), *ca.* late summer 1942.
Engine: One 785/820 h.p. Bristol Mercury XX or 30 radial. *Span:* 39 ft. 0 in.
(11·89 m.). *Length:* 30 ft. 11 in. (9·42 m.). *Height:* 11 ft. 7 in. (3·53 m.). *Normal
take-off weight:* 6,680 lb. (3,030 kg.). *Maximum speed:* 237 m.p.h. (381 km./
hr.) at 15,000 ft. (4,572 m.). *Normal range:* approximately 600 miles (966 km.).
Armament: None.

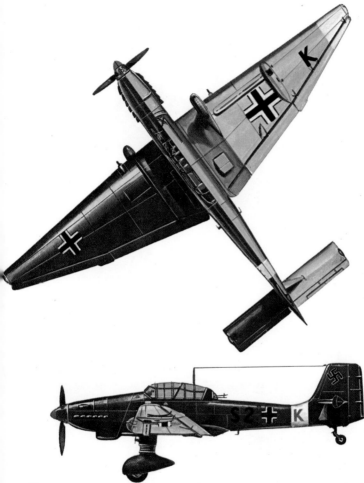

JUNKERS Ju 87 (Germany)

35

Junkers Ju 87D-3 of 2/St. G. 77, Eastern Front summer 1943. *Engine:* One 1,400 h.p. Junkers Jumo 211J-1 inverted-Vee type. *Span:* 45 ft. 3¼ in. (13·80 m.). *Length:* 37 ft. 8¾ in. (11·50 m.). *Height:* 12 ft. 9⅛ in. (3·89 m.). *Maximum take-off weight:* 14,550 lb. (6,600 kg.). *Maximum speed:* 255 m.p.h. (410 km./hr.) at 13,500 ft. (4,115 m.). *Operational ceiling:* 15,520 ft. (4,730 m.). *Maximum range:* 954 miles (1,535 km.). *Armament:* One 7·9 mm. MG 17 machine-gun in each wing and two 7·9 mm. MG 81 guns in rear cockpit; typical warload of one 1,102 lb. (500 kg.) bomb beneath fuselage and one pack of ninety-two 4·4 lb. (2 kg.) SC-2 anti-personnel bombs beneath each wing.

FAIRCHILD PT-19 (U.S.A.)

36

Fairchild PT-19A of the U.S.A.A.F., 1941–42. *Engine:* One 200 h.p. Ranger L-440-3 inverted in-line. *Span:* 35 ft. 11⅞ in. (10·97 m.). *Length:* 28 ft. 0 in. (8·53 m.). *Height:* 10 ft. 6 in. (3·20 m.). *Normal take-off weight:* 2,545 lb. (1,154 kg.). *Maximum speed:* 132 m.p.h. (212 km./hr.) at sea level. *Operational ceiling:* 15,300 ft. (4,663 m.). *Normal range:* 430 miles (692 km.). *Armament:* None.

37

Miles Magister I (impressed civil aircraft) of the R.A.F. (unit unidentified), 1941.
Engine: One 130 h.p. de Havilland Gipsy Major 1 inverted-Vee type. *Span:*
33 ft. 10 in. (10·31 m.). *Length:* 24 ft. 7½ in. (7·51 m.). *Height:* 9 ft. 1 in.
(2·77 m.). *Normal take-off weight:* 1,863 lb. (845 kg.). *Maximum speed:*
132 m.p.h. (212 km./hr.) at 1,000 ft. (305 m.). *Operational ceiling:* 18,000 ft.
(5,486 m.). *Normal range:* 380 miles (612 km.). *Armament:* None.

ILYUSHIN II-2 (U.S.S.R.)

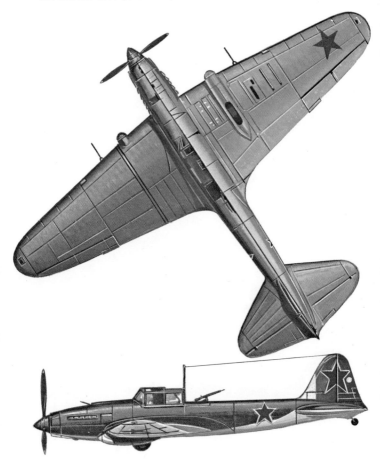

38

Ilyushin II-2m3 *Shturmovik* of the VVS-RKKA (Soviet Air Force), Eastern Front 1944. *Engine:* One 1,770 h.p. Mikulin AM-38F Vee type. *Span:* 47 ft. 10¾ in. (14·60 m.). *Length:* 38 ft. 2⅝ in. (11·65 m.). *Height:* 11 ft. 1⅞ in. (3·40 m.). *Normal take-off weight:* 12,147 lb. (5,510 kg.). *Maximum speed:* 251 m.p.h. (404 km./hr.) at 4,920 ft. (1,500 m.). *Operational ceiling:* 19,685 ft. (6,000 m.). *Normal range:* 373 miles (600 km.). *Armament:* One 23 mm. VYa cannon in each wing, two 7·62 mm. ShKAS machine-guns in upper front fuselage, and one 12·7 mm. UBT machine-gun in rear cockpit; provision for 882 lb. (400 kg.) of bombs internally and four 82 mm. RS-82 rocket projectiles or an additional 220 lb. (100 kg.) of bombs beneath each wing.

39

Boulton Paul Defiant I of No. 256 Squadron R.A.F., U.K. October 1941. *Engine:* One 1,030 h.p. Rolls-Royce Merlin III Vee type. *Span:* 39 ft. 4 in. (11·99 m.). *Length:* 35 ft. 4 in. (10·77 m.). *Height:* 12 ft. 2 in. (3·71 m.). *Normal take-off weight:* 8,318 lb. (3,773 kg.). *Maximum speed:* 304 m.p.h. (489 km./hr.) at 17,000 ft. (5,182 m.). *Operational ceiling:* 30,350 ft. (9,251 m.). *Normal range:* 465 miles (748 km.). *Armament:* Four 0·303 in. Browning machine-guns in dorsal turret.

DEWOITINE D. 520 (France)

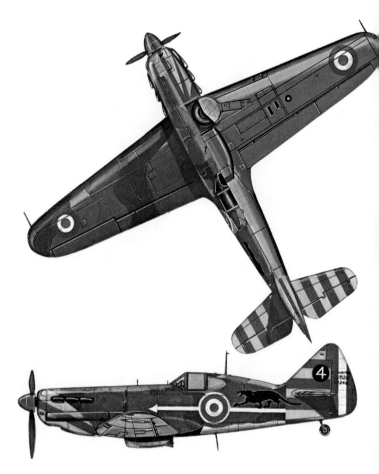

40

Dewoitine D. 520 of GC.II/7 (4th *Escadrille*), Vichy Air Force, Tunisia early 1942. *Engine:* One 930 h.p. Hispano-Suiza 12Y-45 Vee type. *Span:* 33 ft. 5⅝ in. (10·20 m.). *Length:* 28 ft. 8⅞ in. (8·76 m.). *Height:* 8 ft. 5⅛ in. (2·57 m.). *Maximum take-off weight:* 6,135 lb. (2,783 kg.). *Maximum speed:* 326 m.p.h. (525 km./hr.) at 19,685 ft. (6,000 m.). *Operational ceiling:* 36,090 ft. (11,000 m.). *Normal range:* 615 miles (990 km.). *Armament:* One 20 mm. Hispano HS 404 cannon mounted in the engine Vee and firing through the propeller hub, and two 7·5 mm. MAC 1934-M39 machine-guns in each wing.

41

Miles Master I of the R.A.F. (unit unidentified), *ca.* early summer 1942. *Engine:*
One 715 h.p. Rolls-Royce Kestrel XXX Vee type. *Span* (originally)*:* 39 ft. 0 in.
(11·89 m.). *Span* (as illustrated)*:* 35 ft. 7 in. (10·85 m.). *Length:* 30 ft. 5 in.
(9·27 m.). *Height:* 9 ft. 3 in. (2·82 m.). *Normal take-off weight:* 5,352 lb.
(2,428 kg.). *Maximum speed:* 226 m.p.h. (364 km./hr.) at 15,000 ft. (4,572 m.).
Operational ceiling: 28,000 ft. (8,534 m.). *Normal range:* 500 miles (805 km.).
Armament: Provision for one 0·303 in. Vickers machine-gun in upper front
fuselage and eight practice bombs beneath wing centre-section.

YAKOVLEV Yak-9 (U.S.S.R.)

42

Yakovlev Yak-9D of a Soviet Air Force Guards Fighter Regiment, Crimea, spring 1944. *Engine:* One 1,210 h.p. Klimov M-105 PF Vee type. *Span:* 32 ft. 9¾ in. (10·00 m.). *Length:* 28 ft. 0⅝ in. (8·55 m.). *Height:* 9 ft. 10⅛ in. (3·00 m.). *Normal take-off weight:* 6,867 lb. (3,115 kg.). *Maximum speed:* 373 m.p.h. (600 km./hr.) at 11,485 ft. (3,500 m.). *Operational ceiling:* 32,810 ft. (10,000 m.). *Normal range:* 808 miles (1,300 km.). *Armament:* One 20 mm. MPSh cannon mounted in the engine Vee and firing through the propeller hub, and one 12·7 mm. UBS machine-gun in port side of the upper front fuselage.

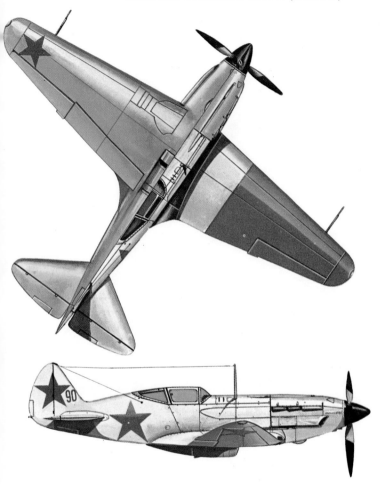

43

Mikoyan-Gurevich MiG-3 of the 12th Fighter Regiment Soviet Air Force, Northern Front, winter 1941–42. *Engine:* One 1,350 h.p. Mikulin AM-35A Vee type. *Span:* 33 ft. 9½ in. (10·30 m.). *Length:* 26 ft. 9 in. (8·155 m.). *Height:* approximately 11 ft. 6 in. (3·50 m.). *Normal take-off weight:* 7,242 lb. (3,285 kg.). *Maximum speed:* 398 m.p.h. (640 km./hr.) at 22,965 ft. (7,000 m.). *Operational ceiling:* 39,370 ft. (12,000 m.). *Normal range:* 510 miles (820 km.). *Armament:* One 12·7 mm. Beresin BS machine-gun and two 7·62 mm. ShKAS machine-guns in upper front fuselage; provision for one 220 lb. (100 kg.) bomb, two 55 lb. (25 kg.) bombs or three 82 mm. RS-82 rocket projectiles beneath each wing.

MUSTANG (U.S.A.)

44

North American P-51D-5-NA of the 339th Fighter Group, 66th Fighter Wing U.S. Eighth Air Force, interned in Sweden August 1944 and later purchased by the R.Sw.A.F. *Engine:* One 1,490 h.p. Packard-built V-1650-7 (Rolls-Royce Merlin) Vee type. *Span:* 37 ft. 0¼ in. (11·29 m.). *Length:* 32 ft. 3¼ in. (9·84 m.). *Height:* 13 ft. 8 in. (4·16 m.). *Normal take-off weight:* 10,100 lb. (4,581 kg.). *Maximum speed:* 437 m.p.h. (703 km./hr.) at 25,000 ft. (7,620 m.). *Operational ceiling:* 41,900 ft. (12,771 m.). *Normal range:* 950 miles (1,529 km.). *Armament:* Three 0·50 in. Browning MG 53-2 machine-guns in each wing; provision (with two guns deleted) for one 1,000 lb. (454 kg.) bomb, five 5 in. rocket projectiles or three bazooka-type rocket launching tubes beneath each wing.

KAWASAKI Ki-61 (Japan)

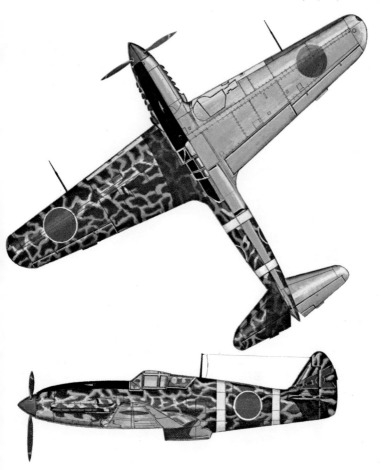

45

Kawasaki Ki-61-Ib Model 1B *Hien* of the 68th Fighter Group J.A.A.F., New Britain *ca.* spring 1944. *Engine:* One 1,175 h.p. Kawasaki Ha-40 inverted-Vee type. *Span:* 39 ft. 4½ in. (12·00 m.). *Length:* 28 ft. 8½ in. (8·75 m.). *Height:* 12 ft. 1⅝ in. (3·70 m.). *Normal take-off weight:* 6,504 lb. (2,950 kg.). *Maximum speed:* 368 m.p.h. (592 km./hr.) at 15,945 ft. (4,860 m.). *Operational ceiling:* 38,060 ft. (11,600 m.). *Normal range:* 373 miles (600 km.). *Armament:* Two 12·7 mm. Type 1 machine-guns in upper front fuselage and one in each wing.

HURRICANE (U.K.)

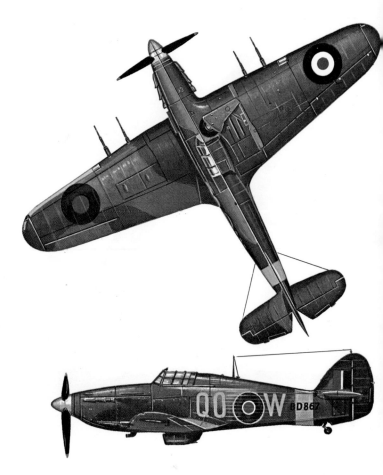

46

Hawker Hurricane IIC of No. 3 Squadron R.A.F., U.K. 1941. *Engine:* One 1,300 h.p. Rolls-Royce Merlin XX Vee type. *Span:* 40 ft. 0 in. (12·19 m.). *Length:* 32 ft. 2¼ in. (9·81 m.). *Height:* 13 ft. 1 in. (3·99 m.). *Normal take-off weight:* 7,544 lb. (3,422 kg.). *Maximum speed:* 329 m.p.h. (529 km./hr.) at 18,000 ft. (5,486 m.). *Operational ceiling:* 35,600 ft. (10,851 m.). *Normal range:* 460 miles (740 km.). *Armament:* Two 20 mm. Oerlikon or Hispano cannon in each wing; provision for one 250 lb. (113 kg.) or 500 lb. (227 kg.) bomb beneath each wing.

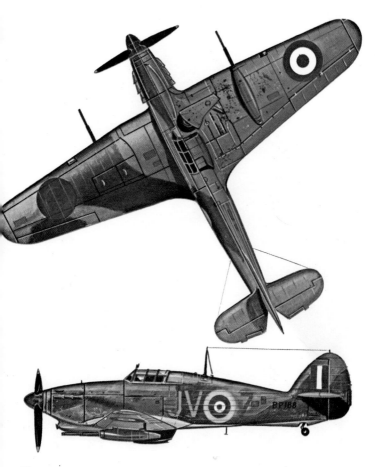

47

Hawker Hurricane IID of No. 6 Squadron R.A.F., Middle East 1942. *Engine:* One 1,300 h.p. Rolls-Royce Merlin XX Vee type. *Span:* 40 ft. 0 in. (12·19 m.). *Length:* 32 ft. 2¼ in. (9·81 m.). *Height:* 13 ft. 1 in. (3·99 m.). *Maximum take-off weight:* 8,100 lb. (3,674 kg.). *Maximum speed:* 316 m.p.h. (509 km./hr.) at 19,000 ft. (5,791 m.). *Operational ceiling:* 33,500 ft. (10,211 m.). *Range:* 480 miles (772 km.). *Armament:* One 0·303 in. Browning machine-gun in each wing and one 40 mm. Vickers S cannon in fairing beneath each wing.

MESSERSCHMITT Bf 109 (Germany)

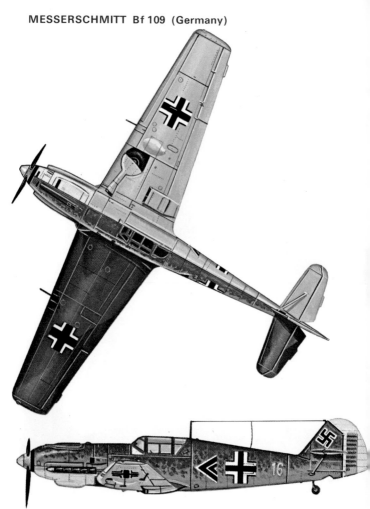

48

Messerschmitt Bf 109E-4 flown by Major Adolf Galland while commanding III/JG.26, France, June 1941. *Engine:* One 1,150 h.p. Daimler-Benz DB 601Aa inverted-Vee type. *Span:* 32 ft. 4½ in. (9·87 m.). *Length:* 28 ft. 4⅛ in. (8·64 m.). *Height:* 11 ft. 1⅞ in. (3·40 m.). *Normal take-off weight:* 5,523 lb. (2,505 kg.). *Maximum speed:* 357 m.p.h. (575 km./hr.) at 12,305 ft. (3,750 m.). *Operational ceiling:* 36,090 ft. (11,000 m.). *Normal range:* 413 miles (665 km.). *Armament:* Two 7·9 mm. MG 17 machine-guns in upper front fuselage and one 20 mm. MG FF cannon in each wing.

49

Macchi C.202 *Serie* XI *Folgore* of the 353° *Squadriglia*, 20° *Gruppo*, 51° *Stormo C.T.,* Monserrato (Italy) *ca.* July 1943. *Engine:* One 1,075 h.p. Alfa Romeo R.A.1000 RC 41 (licence-built DB 601A-1) inverted-Vee type. *Span:* 34 ft. 8½ in. (10·58 m.). *Length:* 29 ft. 0⅜ in. (8·85 m.). *Height:* 9 ft. 11¼ in. (3·03 m.). *Normal take-off weight:* 6,459 lb. (2,930 kg.). *Maximum speed:* 370 m.p.h. (595 km./hr.) at 19,685 ft. (6,000 m.). *Operational ceiling:* 37,730 ft. (11,500 m.). *Normal range:* 475 miles (765 km.). *Armament:* Two 12·7 mm. Breda-SAFAT machine-guns in upper front fuselage and one 7·7 mm. Breda-SAFAT machine-gun in each wing.

KINGCOBRA (U.S.A.)

50

Bell P-63A-6 Kingcobra of the Soviet Air Force, *ca.* 1944. *Engine:* One 1,325 h.p. Allison V-1710-95 Vee type. *Span:* 38 ft. 4 in. (11·68 m.). *Length:* 32 ft. 8 in. (9·96 m.). *Height:* 12 ft. 7 in. (3·84 m.). *Normal take-off weight:* 8,800 lb. (3,992 kg.). *Maximum speed:* 408 m.p.h. (657 km./hr.) at 24,450 ft. (7,452 m.). *Operational ceiling:* 43,000 ft. (13,105 m.). *Typical range:* 450 miles (724 km.). *Armament:* One 37 mm. cannon firing through the propeller hub, two 0·50 in. machine-guns in upper front fuselage and one in each wing; provision for one 500 lb. (227 kg.) bomb beneath fuselage and one beneath each wing.

51

Bell P-39D Airacobra of the 35th Fighter Group U.S.A.A.F., New Guinea 1942.
Engine: One 1,150 h.p. Allison V-1710-35 Vee type. *Span:* 34 ft. 0 in. (10·36 m.).
Length: 29 ft. 9 in. (9·07 m.). *Height:* 11 ft. 10 in. (3·61 m.). *Normal take-off
weight:* 7,650 lb. (3,470 kg.). *Maximum speed:* 368 m.p.h. (592 km./hr.) at
13,800 ft. (4,206 m.). *Operational ceiling:* 32,100 ft. (9,784 m.). *Normal range:*
800 miles (1,287 km.). *Armament:* One 37 mm. cannon firing through the
propeller hub, two 0·50 in. Browning M-2 machine-guns in upper front
fuselage and two 0·30 in. machine-guns in each wing; provision for one 500 lb.
(227 kg.) bomb beneath fuselage.

TYPHOON (U.K.)

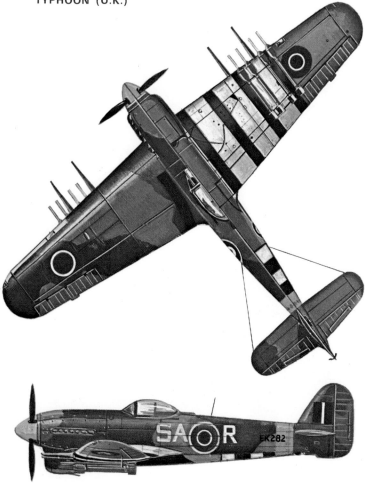

52

Hawker Typhoon IB of No. 486 Squadron R.N.Z.A.F., U.K. summer 1944. *Engine:* One 2,200 h.p. Napier Sabre IIB in-line. *Span:* 41 ft. 7 in. (12·67 m.). *Length:* 31 ft. 10¾ in. (9·72 m.). *Height:* 14 ft. 10 in. (4·52 m.). *Maximum take-off weight:* 12,905 lb. (5,853 kg.). *Maximum speed:* 409 m.p.h. (658 km./hr.) at 10,000 ft. (3,048 m.). *Operational ceiling:* 34,000 ft. (10,363 m.). *Range with underwing drop-tanks:* 910 miles (1,465 km.). *Armament:* Two 20 mm. Hispano cannon in each wing; provision for one 1,000 lb. (454 kg.) bomb or four 60 lb. (27 kg.) rocket projectiles beneath each wing.

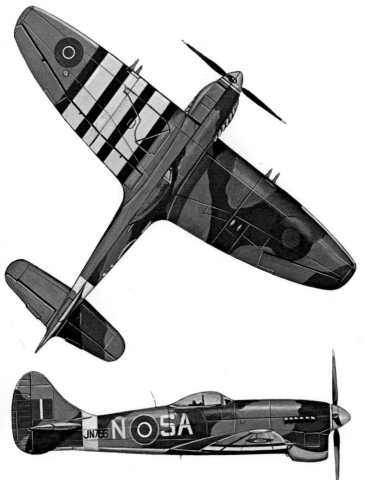

53

Hawker Tempest V Series 1 of No. 486 Squadron R.N.Z.A.F., U.K. *ca.* late spring 1944. *Engine:* One 2,180 h.p. Napier Sabre IIA in-line. *Span:* 41 ft. 0 in. (12·50 m.). *Length:* 33 ft. 8 in. (10·26 m.). *Height:* 16 ft. 1 in. (4·90 m.). *Normal take-off weight:* 11,500 lb. (5,217 kg.). *Maximum speed:* 436 m.p.h. (701 km./hr.) at 18,500 ft. (5,639 m.). *Operational ceiling:* 36,500 ft. (11,125 m.). *Normal range:* 740 miles (1,191 km.). *Armament:* Two 20 mm. Hispano Mk. II cannon in each wing; provision for one 1,000 lb. (454 kg.) bomb, four 60 lb. (27 kg.) rocket projectiles or other weapons beneath each wing.

FULMAR (U.K.)

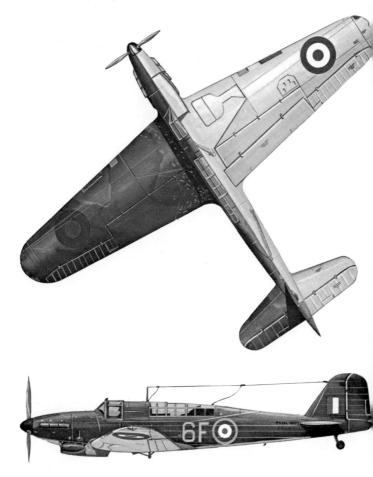

54

Fairey Fulmar II of No. 802 Squadron F.A.A., Malta theatre April 1942. *Engine:* One 1,300 h.p. Rolls-Royce Merlin 30 Vee type. *Span:* 46 ft. 4½ in. (14·14 m.). *Length:* 40 ft. 2 in. (12·24 m.). *Height:* 14 ft. 1¼ in. (4·30 m.). *Normal take-off weight:* 9,672 lb. (4,387 kg.). *Maximum speed:* 272 m.p.h. (438 km./hr.) at 7,250 ft. (2,210 m.). *Operational ceiling:* 27,200 ft. (8,291 m.). *Normal range:* 780 miles (1,255 km.). *Armament:* Four 0·303 in. Browning machine-guns in each wing and provision for one 0·303 in. Vickers K gun in rear cockpit; provision for one 100 or 250 lb. (45 or 113 kg.) bomb beneath each wing.

FIREFLY (U.K.)

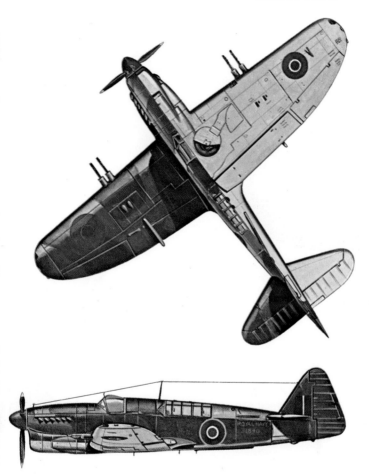

55

Fairey Firefly FR I of No. 1770 Squadron F.A.A., July 1944. *Engine:* One
1,730 h.p. Rolls-Royce Griffon IIB Vee type. *Span:* 44 ft. 6 in. (13·56 m.).
Length: 37 ft. 7¼ in. (11·46 m.). *Height:* 13 ft. 7 in. (4·14 m.). *Maximum take-off
weight:* 14,020 lb. (6,359 kg.). *Maximum speed:* 316 m.p.h. (509 km./hr.) at
14,000 ft. (4,267 m.). *Operational ceiling:* 28,000 ft. (8,534 m.). *Maximum
range with auxiliary tanks:* 1,070 miles (1,722 km.). *Armament:* Two 20 mm.
Hispano cannon in each wing; provision for one 1,000 lb. (454 kg.) bomb or
four 60 lb. (27 kg.) rocket projectiles beneath each wing.

SPITFIRE (U.K.)

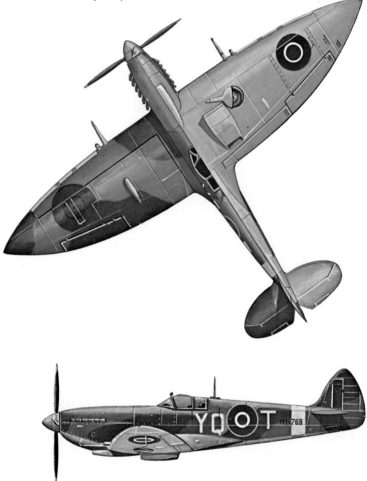

56

Supermarine Spitfire HF VII of No. 616 Squadron R.A.F., U.K. 1942. *Engine:* One 1,710 h.p. Rolls-Royce Merlin 64 Vee type. *Span:* 40 ft. 2 in. (12·24 m.). *Length:* 31 ft. 3½ in. (9·54 m.). *Height:* 12 ft. 7¼ in. (3·68 m.). *Maximum take-off weight:* 7,875 lb. (3,572 kg.). *Maximum speed:* 408 m.p.h. (657 km./hr.) at 25,000 ft. (7,620 m.). *Operational ceiling:* 43,000 ft. (13,106 m.). *Normal range:* 660 miles (1,062 km.). *Armament:* One 20 mm. Hispano cannon and two 0·303 in. Browning machine-guns in each wing.

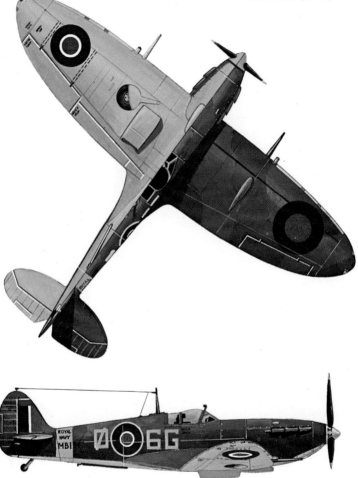

57

Supermarine Seafire F IIC of No. 885 Squadron F.A.A., H.M.S. *Formidable, ca.* September 1942. *Engine:* One 1,470 h.p. Rolls-Royce Merlin 45 Vee type. *Span:* 36 ft. 10 in. (11·53 m.). *Length:* 29 ft. 11 in. (9·12 m.). *Height:* 11 ft. 4¾ in. (3·47 m.). *Maximum take-off weight:* 7,100 lb. (3,220 kg.). *Maximum speed:* 352 m.p.h. (566 km./hr.) at 12,250 ft. (3,734 m.). *Operational ceiling:* 33,800 ft. (10,302 m.). *Normal range:* 465 miles (748 km.). *Armament:* One 20 mm. Hispano cannon and two 0·303 in. Browning machine-guns in each wing; provision for one 500 lb. (227 kg.) bomb beneath the fuselage or one 250 lb. (113 kg.) bomb beneath each wing.

73

WARHAWK (U.S.A.)

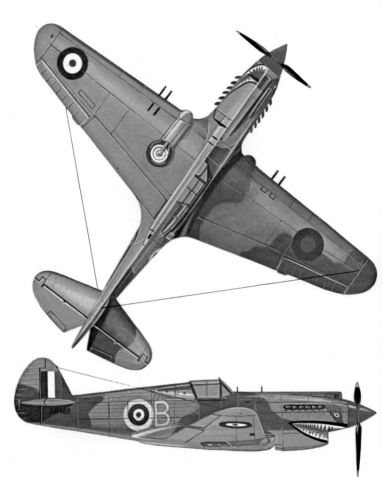

58

Curtiss P-40C Warhawk (Tomahawk IIB) of No. 112 Squadron R.A.F., Egypt autumn 1941. *Engine:* One 1,040 h.p. Allison V-1710-33 Vee type. *Span:* 37 ft. 3½ in. (11·37 m.). *Length:* 31 ft. 8½ in. (9·66 m.). *Height:* 12 ft. 4 in. (3·66 m.). *Normal take-off weight:* 7,549 lb. (3,424 kg.). *Maximum speed:* 345 m.p.h. (555 km./hr.) at 15,000 ft. (4,572 m.). *Operational ceiling:* 29,500 ft. (8,992 m.). *Normal range:* 730 miles (1,175 km.). *Armament:* Two 0·50 in. machine-guns in upper front fuselage and two 0·30 in. guns in each wing.

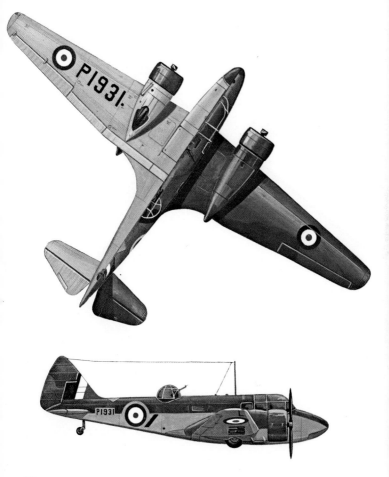

59
Airspeed Oxford I of the R.A.F. (unit unidentified), August 1940. *Engines:* Two 375 h.p. Armstrong Siddeley Cheetah X radials. *Span:* 53 ft. 4 in. (16·26 m.). *Length:* 34 ft. 6 in. (10·52 m.). *Height:* 11 ft. 1 in. (3·38 m.). *Normal take-off weight:* 7,500 lb. (3,402 kg.). *Maximum speed:* 185 m.p.h. (298 km./hr.) at 7,500 ft. (2,286 m.). *Operational ceiling:* 19,500 ft. (5,944 m.). *Normal range:* 960 miles (1,545 km.). *Armament:* None as trainer; some Oxfords on anti-submarine patrols carried 250 lb. (113 kg.) of bombs internally.

HENSCHEL Hs 129 (Germany)

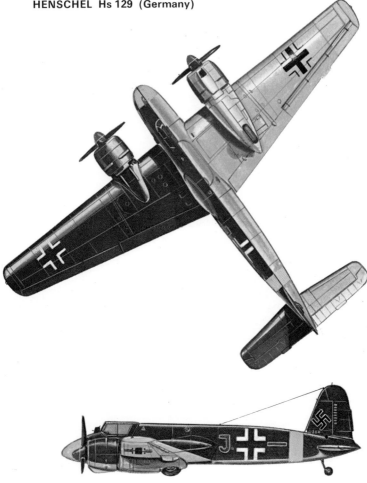

60

Henschel Hs 129B-2/R2 of an unidentified *Schlachtgeschwader*, Eastern Front, late summer 1943. *Engines:* Two 740 h.p. Gnome-Rhône 14M 04/05 radials. *Span:* 46 ft. 7 in. (14·20 m.). *Length:* 31 ft. 11¾ in. (9·75 m.). *Height:* 10 ft. 8 in. (3·25 m.). *Normal take-off weight:* 9,259 lb. (4,200 kg.). *Maximum speed:* 253 m.p.h. (407 km./hr.) at 12,500 ft. (3,810 m.). *Operational ceiling:* 29,530 ft. (9,000 m.). *Normal range:* 429 miles (690 km.). *Armament:* Two 20 mm. MG 151 cannon and two 7·9 mm. MG 17 machine-guns in fuselage nose, and one 30 mm. MK 101 cannon in ventral fairing.

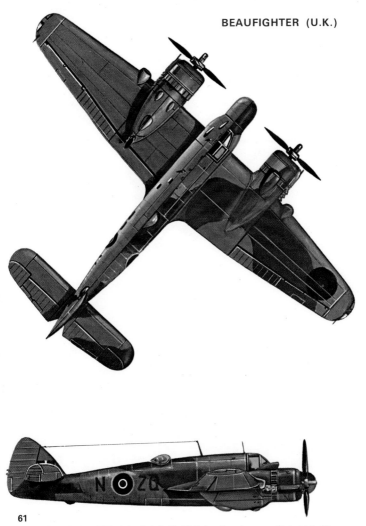

BEAUFIGHTER (U.K.)

61

Bristol Beaufighter VIF of the R.A.F. Air Fighting Development Unit, U.K. May 1944. *Engines:* Two 1,670 h.p. Bristol Hercules VI or XVI radials. *Span:* 57 ft. 10 in. (17·63 m.). *Length:* 41 ft. 8 in. (12·70 m.). *Height:* 15 ft. 10 in. (4·83 m.). *Maximum take-off weight:* 21,600 lb. (9,797 kg.). *Maximum speed:* 333 m.p.h. (536 km./hr.) at 15,600 ft. (4,755'm.). *Operational ceiling:* 26,500 ft. (8,077 m.). *Normal range:* 1,480 miles (2,382 km.). *Armament:* Four 20 mm. Hispano cannon in fuselage nose and three 0·303 in. Browning machine-guns in each wing.

JUNKERS Ju 88 (Germany)

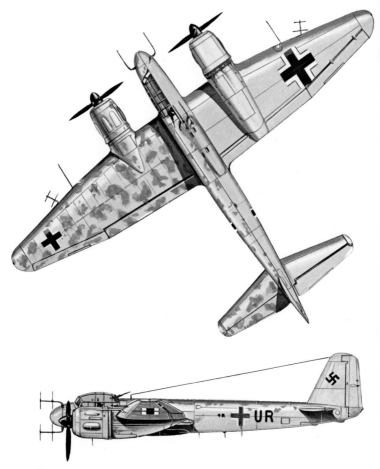

62

Junkers Ju 88G-1 of 7/NJG.2, which fell into Allied hands July 1944. *Engines:* Two 1,700 h.p. BMW 801D radials. *Span:* 65 ft. 7¾ in. (20·00 m.). *Length:* 54 ft. 1½ in. (16·50 m.). *Height:* 15 ft. 11 in. (4·85 m.). *Normal take-off weight:* 28,880 lb. (13,100 kg.). *Maximum speed:* 342 m.p.h. (550 km./hr.) at 27,890 ft. (8,500 m.). *Operational ceiling:* 32,480 ft. (9,900 m.). *Typical range:* 1,553 miles (2,500 km.). *Armament:* Four 20 mm. MG 151 cannon in ventral pack and one 13 mm. MG 131 machine-gun in rear of cabin.

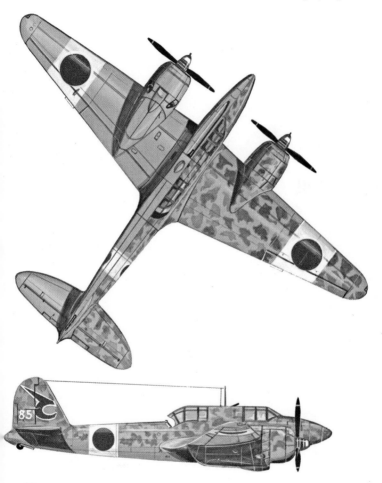

63

Kawasaki Ki-45-KAIc of the 2nd Squadron, 53rd Group J.A.A.F., Chiba Prefecture, home defence of Japan late 1944. *Engines:* Two 1,080 h.p. Mitsubishi Ha-102 radials. *Span:* 49 ft. 3¾ in. (15·02 m.). *Length:* 36 ft. 1⅛ in. (11·00 m.). *Height:* 12 ft. 1⅝ in. (3·70 m.). *Normal take-off weight:* 12,125 lb. (5,500 kg.). *Maximum speed:* 340 m.p.h. (547 km./hr.) at 21,325 ft. (6,500 m.). *Operational ceiling:* 32,810 ft. (10,000 m.). *Maximum range:* 1,243 miles (2,000 km.). *Armament:* One 37 mm. Ho-203 cannon in ventral tunnel, two 20 mm. Ho-5 cannon in dorsal position and one 7·92 mm. Type 98 machine-gun in rear cockpit.

NAKAJIMA J1N (Japan)

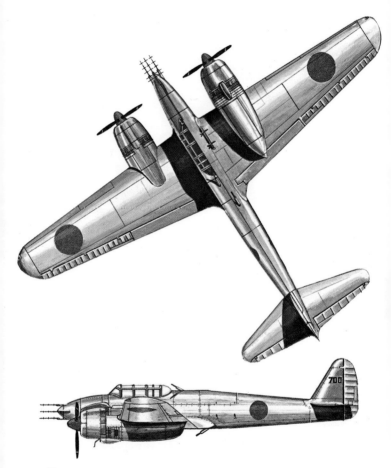

64

Nakajima J1N1-S, captured aircraft displayed in the U.S.A. *ca.* late 1945. *Engines:* Two 1,130 h.p. Nakajima Sakae 21 radials. *Span:* 55 ft. 8½ in. (16·98 m.). *Length* (excluding aerials): 39 ft. 11½ in. (12·18 m.). *Height:* 14 ft. 11½ in. (4·56 m.). *Normal take-off weight:* 15,212 lb. (6,900 kg.). *Maximum speed:* 315 m.p.h. (507 km./hr.) at 19,160 ft. (5,840 m.). *Operational ceiling:* 30,580 ft. (9,320 m.). *Normal range:* 1,584 miles (2,550 km.). *Armament:* Two 20 mm. Type 99-II cannon in dorsal position and two in ventral position.

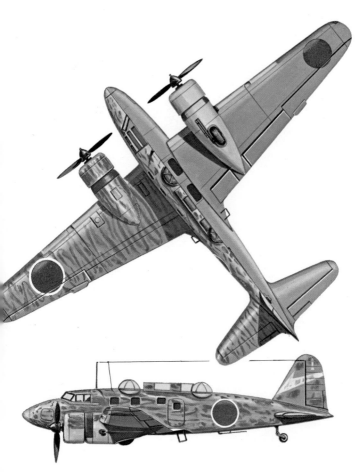

65

Tachikawa Ki-54 of the J.A.A.F. (unit unidentified), late 1944. *Engines:* Two 515 h.p. Nakajima Ha-13 Kotobuki radials. *Span:* 58 ft. 0⅞ in. (17·70 m.). *Length:* 39 ft. 0½ in. (11·90 m.). *Height:* 11 ft. 9 in. (3·58 m.). *Normal take-off weight:* 8,995 lb. (4,080 kg.). *Maximum speed:* 228 m.p.h. (367 km./hr.) at 6,560 ft. (2,000 m.). *Operational ceiling:* 19,390 ft. (5,910 m.). *Typical range:* 435 miles (700 km.). *Armament:* None.

POTEZ 63 (France)

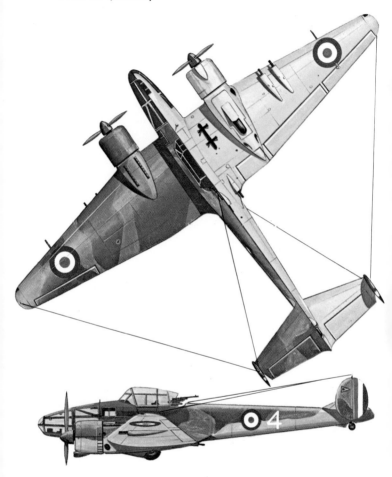

66

Potez P.63-11 of GR.II/39 (3rd *Escadrille*), Syria 1941. *Engines:* Two 700 h.p. Gnome-Rhône 14M series radials. *Span:* 52 ft. 5⅞ in. (16·00 m.). *Length:* 36 ft. 1¼ in. (11·004 m.). *Height:* 11 ft. 10½ in. (3·62 m.). *Normal take-off weight:* 9,773 lb. (4,433 kg.). *Maximum speed:* 264 m.p.h. (425 km./hr.) at 16,405 ft. (5,000 m.). *Operational ceiling:* 29,530 ft. (9,000 m.). *Maximum range:* 932 miles (1,500 km.). *Armament:* Two 7·5 mm. MAC 1934 machine-guns beneath each wing, one in rear cockpit and three in ventral position; provision for eight 22 lb. (10 kg.) bombs internally and two 110 lb. (50 kg.) bombs beneath each wing.

HEINKEL He 219 (Germany)

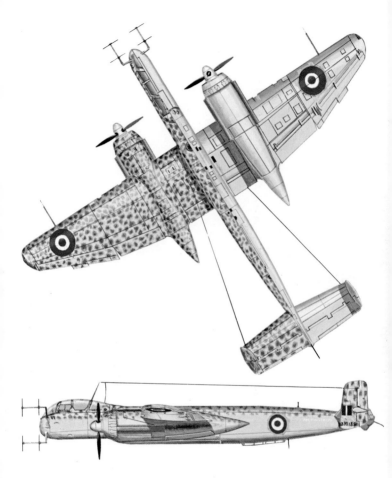

67

Heinkel He 219A-5/R2 *Uhu*, captured aircraft with R.A.F. markings super-imposed, *ca.* late autumn 1945. *Engines:* Two 1,800 h.p. Daimler-Benz DB 603E inverted-Vee type. *Span:* 60 ft. 8⅜ in. (18·50 m.). *Length:* 51 ft. 0¼ in. (15·55 m.). *Height:* 13 ft. 5⅝ in. (4·10 m.). *Maximum take-off weight:* 33,730 lb. (15,300 kg.). *Maximum speed:* 416 m.p.h. (670 km./hr.) at 22,965 ft. (7,000 m.). *Operational ceiling:* 39,600 ft. (12,700 m.). *Maximum range:* 1,243 miles (2,000 km.). *Armament:* Four 20 mm. MG 151 cannon in ventral pack and one in each wing root.

DORNIER Do 217 (Germany)

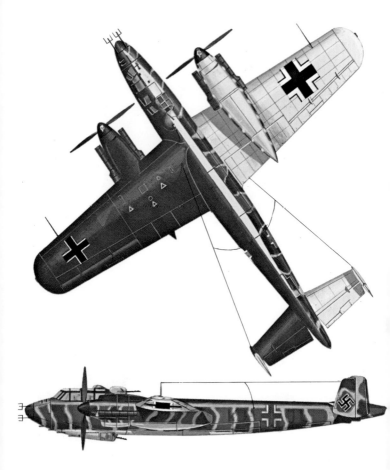

68

Dornier Do 217N-1 of an unidentified *Nachtjagdgeschwader, ca.* spring 1943. *Engines:* Two 1,750 h.p. Daimler-Benz DB 603A inverted-Vee type. *Span:* 62 ft. 4 in. (19·00 m.). *Length:* 58 ft. 9 in. (17·91 m.). *Height:* 16 ft. 3 in. (4·95 m.). *Normal take-off weight:* 29,101 lb. (13,200 kg.). *Maximum speed:* 320 m.p.h. (515 km./hr.) at 18,700 ft. (5,700 m.). *Operational ceiling:* 29,200 ft. (8,900 m.). *Maximum range:* 1,553 miles (2,500 km.). *Armament:* Four 20 mm. MG 151 cannon and four 7·9 mm. MG 17 machine-guns in fuselage nose, one 13 mm. MG 131 machine-gun in turret aft of cabin and one in rear of ventral cupola.

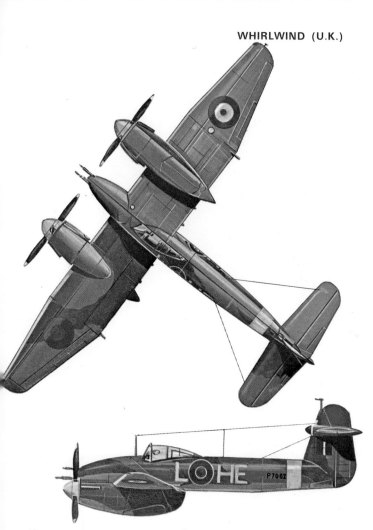

69

Westland Whirlwind I of No. 263 Squadron R.A.F., U.K. summer 1942. *Engines:*
Two 765 h.p. Rolls-Royce Peregrine I Vee type. *Span:* 45 ft. 0 in. (13·72 m.).
Length: 31 ft. 6 in. (9·60 m.). *Height:* 11 ft. 7 in. (3·53 m.). *Normal take-off
weight:* 10,356 lb. (4,697 kg.). *Maximum speed:* 360 m.p.h. (579 km./hr.) at
15,000 ft. (4,572 m.). *Operational ceiling:* 30,000 ft. (9,144 m.). *Maximum
range:* approximately 1,000 miles (1,610 km.). *Armament:* Four 20 mm. Hispano
cannon in fuselage nose; provision for one 250 or 500 lb. (113 or 227 kg.)
bomb beneath each wing.

MOSQUITO (U.K.)

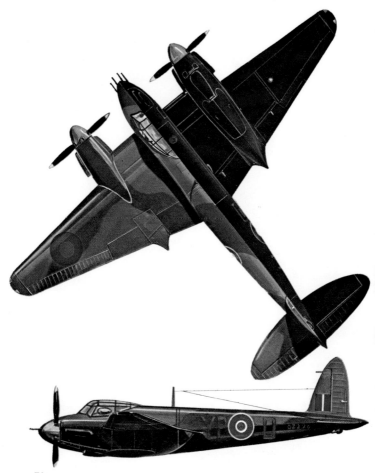

70

De Havilland Mosquito NF II of No. 23 Squadron R.A.F., Malta, January 1943.
Engines: Two 1,460 h.p. Rolls-Royce Merlin 21/23 Vee type. *Span:* 54 ft. 2 in.
(16·51 m.). *Length:* 40 ft. 4 in. (12·29 m.). *Height:* 15 ft. 3½ in. (4·66 m.).
Normal take-off weight: 18,100 lb. (8,210 kg.). *Maximum speed:* 354 m.p.h.
(570 km./hr.) at 14,000 ft. (4,267 m.). *Operational ceiling:* 34,500 ft.
(10,515 m.). *Normal range:* 1,520 miles (2,446 km.). *Armament:* Four 20 mm.
Hispano cannon in lower front fuselage and four 0·303 in. Browning machine-
guns in fuselage nose.

MESSERSCHMITT Me 410 (Germany)

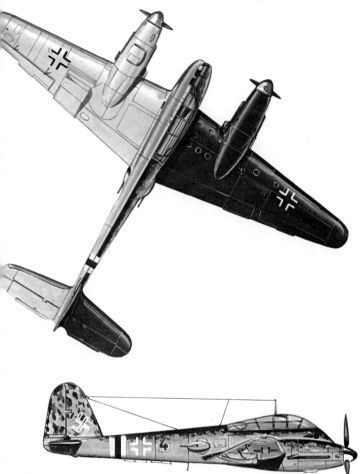

71

Messerschmitt Me 410A-1 *Hornisse* of III/ZG.1 *Wespen*, Germany 1944-45. *Engines:* Two 1,750 h.p. Daimler-Benz DB 603A inverted-Vee type. *Span:* 53 ft. 7¾ in. (16·35 m.). *Length:* 40 ft. 11⅛ in. (12·48 m.). *Height:* 14 ft. 0½ in. (4·28 m.). *Maximum take-off weight:* 23,500 lb. (10,660 kg.). *Maximum speed:* 388 m.p.h. (625 km./hr.) at 21,980 ft. (6,700 m.). *Operational ceiling:* 32,810 ft. (10,000 m.). *Maximum range:* 1,448 miles (2,330 km.). *Armament:* Two 20 mm. MG 151 cannon and two 7·9 mm. MG 17 machine-guns in fuselage nose, and one 13 mm. MG 131 gun in each lateral barbette; provision for up to 4,409 lb. (2,000 kg.) of bombs internally, or 882 lb. (400 kg.) internally and two 110 lb. (50 kg.) bombs beneath each wing root.

MESSERSCHMITT Bf 110 (Germany)

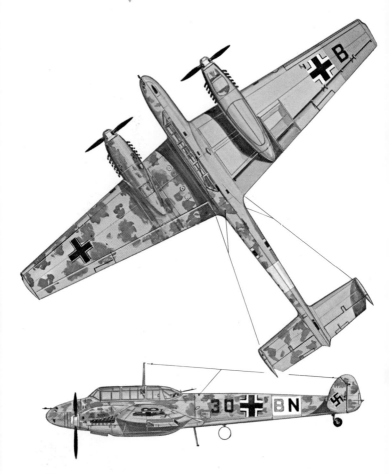

72

Messerschmitt Bf 110C-1 of 5/ZG.26, North Africa 1942. *Engines:* Two 1,100 h.p. Daimler-Benz DB 601A-1 inverted-Vee type. *Span:* 53 ft. 3¾ in. (16·25 m.). *Length:* 39 ft. 7¼ in. (12·07 m.). *Height:* 13 ft. 6⅝ in. (4·13 m.). *Normal take-off weight:* 13,289 lb. (6,028 kg.). *Maximum speed:* 336 m.p.h. (540 km./hr.) at 19,685 ft. (6,000 m.). *Operational ceiling:* 32,810 ft. (10,000 m.). *Maximum range:* 876 miles (1,410 km.). *Armament:* Two 20 mm. MG FF cannon and four 7·9 mm. MG 17 machine-guns in fuselage nose, and one 7·9 mm. MG 15 gun in rear cockpit.

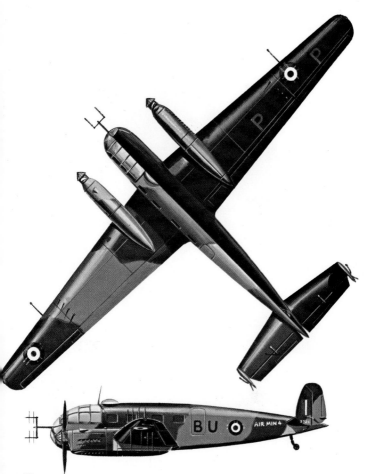

73

Siebel Si 204D-1, captured aircraft with manufacturer's flight test codes and
R.A.F. markings superimposed, autumn 1945. *Engines:* Two 580 h.p. Argus
As 411A-1 inverted-Vee type. *Span:* 69 ft. 10⅝ in. (21·30 m.). *Length:*
39 ft. 0½ in. (11·90 m.). *Height:* 14 ft. 5¼ in. (4·40 m.). *Maximum take-off
weight:* 12,324 lb. (5,590 kg.). *Maximum speed:* 229 m.p.h. (368 km./hr.) at
7,610 ft. (2,320 m.). *Operational ceiling:* 24,605 ft. (7,500 m.). *Maximum range:*
932 miles (1,500 km.). *Armament:* None.

FOKKER G.I (Netherlands)

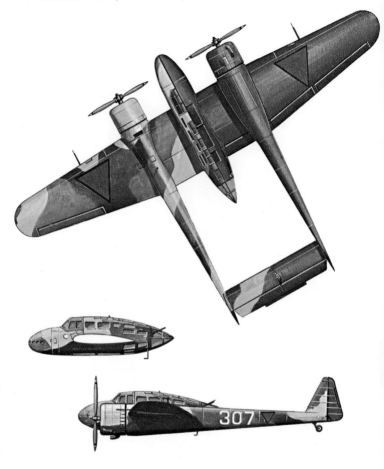

74

Fokker G.IA of the 3rd Fighter Group, 1st Air Regiment LVA, Waalhaven, late 1939. *Engines:* Two 830 h.p. Bristol Mercury VIII radials. *Span:* 56 ft. 3¼ in. (17·15 m.). *Length:* 37 ft. 8¾ in. (11·50 m.). *Height:* 11 ft. 1⅞ in. (3·40 m.). *Normal take-off weight:* 10,582 lb. (4,800 kg.). *Maximum speed:* 295 m.p.h. (475 km./hr.) at 9,020 ft. (2,750 m.). *Operational ceiling:* 30,510 ft. (9,300 m.). *Normal range:* 876 miles (1,410 km.). *Armament:* Eight 7·9 mm. FN-Browning machine-guns in nose of nacelle and one in rear of nacelle; provision for up to 661 lb. (300 kg.) of bombs internally and externally.

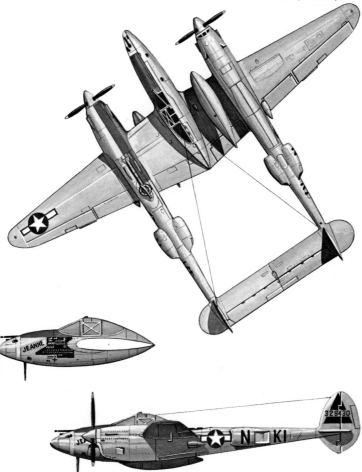

75

Lockheed P-38J-15-LO Lightning of the 55th Fighter Squadron, 20th Fighter Group, U.S. Eighth Air Force, U.K. early 1944. *Engines:* Two 1,425 h.p. Allison V-1710-89/91 Vee type. *Span:* 52 ft. 0 in. (15·85 m.). *Length:* 37 ft. 10 in. (11·53 m.). *Height:* 9 ft. 9¾ in. (2·99 m.). *Normal take-off weight:* 17,500 lb. (7,938 kg.). *Maximum speed:* 414 m.p.h. (666 km/hr.) at 25,000 ft. (7,620 m.). *Operational ceiling:* 44,000 ft. (13,410 m.). *Maximum range on internal fuel:* 1,175 miles (1,891 km.). *Armament:* One 20 mm. Hispano M2 cannon and four 0·50 in. Colt-Browning MG 53-2 machine-guns in nose of nacelle; provision for one bomb of up to 1,600 lb. (726 kg.) size beneath each inboard wing section or five 5 in. rocket projectiles beneath each outer wing section.

SAAB-21 (Sweden)

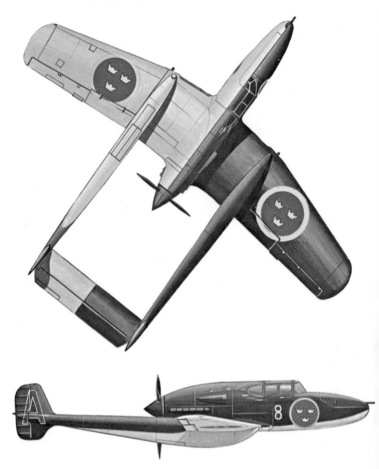

76

Saab J 21A-1 of the 1st Air Division, F 8 Wing Royal Swedish Air Force, Barkarby, *ca.* December 1945. *Engine:* One 1,475 h.p. SFA-built Daimler-Benz DB 605B inverted-Vee type. *Span:* 38 ft. 0⅝ in. (11·60 m.). *Length:* 34 ft. 3¾ in. (10·45 m.). *Height:* 13 ft. 0¼ in. (3·97 m.). *Normal take-off weight:* 9,149 lb. (4,150 kg.). *Maximum speed:* 398 m.p.h. (640 km./hr.) at 16,405 ft. (5,000 m.). *Operational ceiling:* 36,090 ft. (11,000 m.). *Armament:* One 20 mm. Hispano cannon and four 13·2 mm. Hispano machine-guns in nose of nacelle.

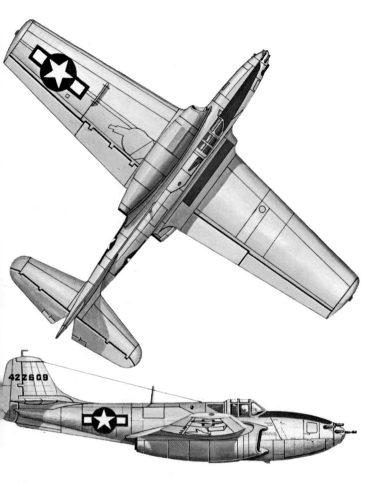

77

Bell P-59A (first production aircraft) of the U.S.A.A.F., Muroc Field late 1943.
Engines: Two 2,000 lb. (907 kg.) st General Electric J31-GE-3 turbojets. *Span:*
45 ft. 6 in. (13·87 m.). *Length:* 38 ft. 1½ in. (11·62 m.). *Height:* 12 ft. 0 in.
(3·66 m.). *Normal take-off weight:* 10,822 lb. (4,909 kg.). *Maximum speed:*
409 m.p.h. (658 km./hr.) at 35,000 ft. (10,668 m.). *Operational ceiling:*
46,200 ft. (14,082 m.). *Normal range:* 240 miles (386 km.). *Armament:* One
37 mm. M4 cannon and three 0·50 in. machine-guns in fuselage nose.

METEOR (U.K.)

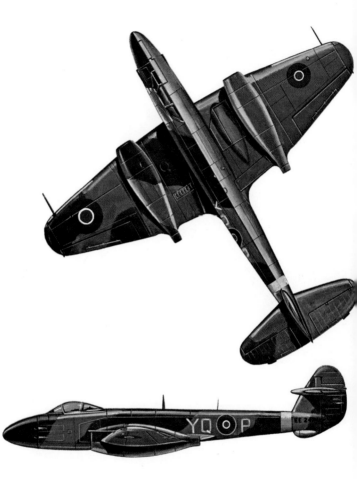

78

Gloster Meteor III of No. 616 Squadron R.A.F., 2nd Allied Tactical Air Force, Germany, January 1945. *Engines:* Two 2,000 lb. (907 kg.) st Rolls-Royce Derwent 1 turbojets. *Span:* 43 ft. 0 in. (13·11 m.). *Length:* 41 ft. 3 in. (12·57 m.). *Height:* 13 ft. 0 in. (3·96 m.). *Maximum take-off weight:* 13,300 lb. (6,033 kg.). *Maximum speed:* 493 m.p.h. (793 km./hr.) at 30,000 ft. (9,144 m.). *Operational ceiling:* 44,000 ft. (13,410 m.). *Maximum range:* 1,340 miles (2,156 km.). *Armament:* Four 20 mm. Hispano Mk. III cannon in fuselage nose.

MESSERSCHMITT Me 262 (Germany)

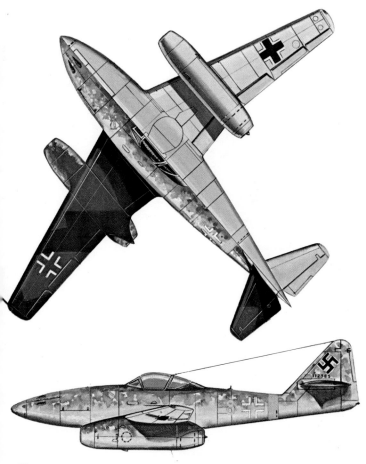

79

Messerschmitt Me 262A-1a *Schwalbe* of 3/JG.7 *Nowotny*, Brandenburg March 1945. *Engines:* Two 1,984 lb. (900 kg.) st Junkers Jumo 004B series turbojets. *Span:* 40 ft. 11½ in. (12·48 m.). *Length:* 34 ft. 9⅜ in. (10·60 m.). *Height:* 12 ft. 7 in. (3·835 m.). *Maximum take-off weight:* 14,101 lb. (6,396 kg.). *Maximum speed:* 541 m.p.h. (870 km./hr.) at 19,685 ft. (6,000 m.). *Operational ceiling:* 37,565 ft. (11,450 m.). *Maximum range:* 652 miles (1,050 km.). *Armament:* Four 30 mm. MK 108 cannon in fuselage nose.

MESSERSCHMITT Me 163 (Germany)

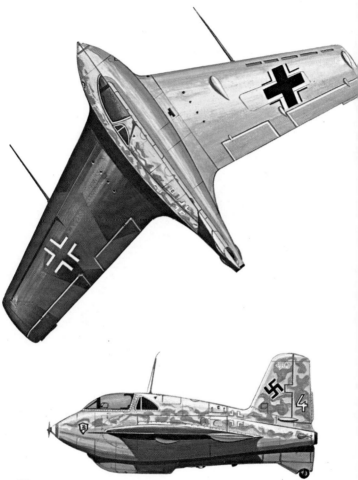

80

Messerschmitt Me 163B-1 *Komet* of 1/JG.400, Zwischenahn, summer 1944. *Engine:* One 3,748 lb. (1,700 kg.) st Walter HWK 109-509A-1 liquid rocket motor. *Span:* 30 ft. 7 in. (9·32 m.). *Length:* 18 ft. 8 in. (5·69 m.). *Height:* 9 ft. 0 in. (2·74 m.). *Normal take-off weight:* 9,502 lb. (4,310 kg.). *Maximum speed:* 597 m.p.h. (960 km./hr.) at 29,500 ft. (9,000 m.). *Operational ceiling:* 39,370 ft. (12,000 m.). *Maximum endurance* (including climb): 8 minutes, after which the aircraft returned to earth in a glide. *Armament:* One 30 mm. MK 108 cannon in each wing root, and four 5 cm. R4M rockets in each wing (firing vertically upward) or twelve R4M rockets beneath each wing firing forward conventionally

De Havilland Tiger Moth

A developed version of the D.H.60 Gipsy Moth, the prototype D.H.82 (G-ABRC) was flown on 26 October 1931, powered by a 120 hp Gipsy III inverted-Vee engine. It soon became the subject of RAF orders, to Specification T.23/31, for *ab initio* training. The initial batch of thirty-five aircraft were designated D.H.60T Tiger Moth I, being followed by an order for fifty aircraft, with 130 hp Gipsy Major 1 engines, designated D.H.82A Tiger Moth II, to Specification 26/33. The Tiger Moth entered service at the RAF Central Flying School in February 1932, and on 3 September 1939 the RAF had over five hundred Tiger Moth II's on strength, plus nearly three hundred examples of the Queen Bee, a radio-controlled target version. To these were soon added substantial numbers of civilian-owned Tiger Moths impressed for war service, and by the time World War 2 ended well over seven thousand Tiger Moths of all kinds had been built, nearly half of them by Morris Motors. Of the remainder, one hundred and fifty-one were built under licence in Norway, Sweden and Portugal, and two thousand nine hundred and forty-nine at factories in the British Commonwealth. Total wartime production for the RAF amounted to four thousand and five Tiger Moth II's, and both this and the Queen Bee were also used in small numbers by the Fleet Air Arm. Two hundred Canadian-built Tiger Moths were supplied in 1942 to the USAAF, by whom they were designated PT-24.

The Tiger Moth was one of the major types utilised in the huge Empire Air Training Scheme, but during the war it was also to be found on miscellaneous other duties that included casualty evacuation and even anti-submarine patrols. It served with the post-war RAF until 1947, and with the RAFVR for a further four years after this, large numbers being 'demobilised' and reappearing in various civil guises from about 1950.

2 Boeing (Stearman) Kaydet series

Various biplanes emanating from the Stearman Aircraft Co (which later became the Wichita Division of the Boeing Aircraft Co) were employed as primary trainers by the US forces before and during World War 2. They stemmed from the 2-seat X70 evaluated by the US Army in 1934–35, after which an initial Army order for twenty-six examples of the Stearman Model 75 was placed in 1936. Delivery of these, under the designation PT-13, began later that year, and by 1942 a further six hundred and sixty-five PT-13A, B, C and D models had also been delivered to the US Army. All were powered by variants of the Lycoming R-680 engine, apart from which they differed in minor detail only. The PT-13D was the first primary trainer to be standardised by both the USAAF and the US Navy, and one thousand four hundred and fifty of this version were built for the Navy as the N2S-5. (The Navy had previously purchased sixty-one Whirlwind-engined Stearman 73's, which it designated NS-1.) Re-engined in 1940 with the 220 hp Continental R-670-5 radial, the PT-13A became known as the PT-17. Three thousand five hundred and nineteen PT-17's were built for the USAAF, and a further quantity for the US Navy, making this the most widely used Kaydet variant. Use of the 225 hp Jacobs R-755-7 engine characterised the PT-18, which also appeared in 1940; one hundred and fifty of this version were completed. The other principal Kaydet type was the PT-27, a 'winterised' version of the PT-17 with enclosed cockpits. Three hundred of these were built in 1942 for Canadian use as part of the Empire Air Training Scheme.

3 Henschel Hs 123

The Henschel Hs 123, the *Luftwaffe*'s first production dive bomber (and also its last combat biplane), first flew in the spring of 1935, making its public debut on 8 May in the hands of General Ernst Udet, the man primarily responsible for its existence. Two of the first three prototypes broke up during high-speed diving tests, but the structural weaknesses were successfully eliminated in the Hs 123V4, which underwent service trials in the autumn of 1935. Apart from the substitution of the more powerful BMW 132Dc radial for the 650 hp BMW 132A-3 of the prototypes, the Hs 123A-1 production model differed little from the V4, and began to enter service with *Luftwaffe* units in mid-1936. In December, five Hs 123's were despatched to Spain to join the Condor Legion and gain genuine battle experience. Others followed in 1938 and, in the event, were used in Spain more for ground-attack duties than for dive-bombing, proving notably successful in their changed role. The decision of the *Luftwaffe* to standardise on the Ju 87 for dive-bombing led to the cessation of Hs 123 production in the autumn of 1938 after only a comparatively small number (by current German standards) had been produced. By 1939 the Hs 123 was virtually obsolete by world standards, but in the early campaigns in Poland, France and the USSR, where the *Luftwaffe*'s air superiority provided a protective umbrella for its activities, it continued to be used with marked success as a close-support aircraft and did not finally disappear from combat units until the summer of 1944; after this it was utilised chiefly for supply dropping or glider towing. Prototypes were flown before the war for proposed Hs 123B and C models the former with a 960 hp BMW 132K engine and the latter a specialised ground-attack version with two extra guns mounted in the wings; but neither of these went into production.

4 Fiat C.R.42 Falco (Falcon)

The C.R.42 marked the culmination of the line of attractive and successful biplane fighters designed for Fiat by Ing Celestino Rosatelli during the 1920s and 1930s, and it was a tribute to their success that the prototype C.R.42 did not fly until early 1939, several years after most other major air forces had trans ferred their affections to monoplane fighters. Nor was the *Regia Aeronautica* its only supporter, for in 1939 thirty-four C.R.42's were ordered for the Belgian Air Force, and fifty exported to Hungary; and in 1940–41 seventy-two were delivered to the Royal Swedish Air Force. The fully retractable tailwheel of the prototype C.R.42 was not retained in production aircraft, but otherwise the design remained basically unchanged. First deliveries were made during 1939, and when Italy entered the war in June 1940 the *Regia Aeronautica* had one hundred and ten Falcos in operational condition and thirty-three more at other bases in Italy. Fifty of these served briefly with the *Corpo Aereo Italiano* in the Brussels area late in 1940, and in their subsequent career the Falcos were employed not only as interceptors but as escort fighters and fighter-bombers in the Mediterranean, North Africa and Italy. Progressively improved versions included the C.R.42*bis*, with four 12·7 mm guns; the 'tropicalised' C.R.42 AS (*Africa Settentrionale* = North Africa); and a version fitted with two 20 mm cannon beneath the lower wings. When used for night fighting, equipped with twin searchlights and radio, the Falco was designated C.R.42 CN (*Caccia Nocturna*). Experimental versions included the twin-float IC.R.42 (I for *Idrovolante* = seaplane), and the C.R.42B which was fitted with a Daimler-Benz DB 601 Vee-type engine. Production of the C.R.42, which ended in 1942, amounted to one thousand seven hundred and

eighty-one aircraft. Despite their quite successful contribution to the Axis war effort, the high loss rate among Italian aircraft is highlighted by the figures for the C.R.42, for when the surrender came on September 1943 the total of Falcos still extant was one hundred and thirteen – thirty less than had been in service in June 1940. The Swedish Falcos (designated J 11) remained in service until 1945, after which a small number were used for a time on civilian target-towing duties.

5 **Gloster Gladiator**

The Gladiator single-seat fighter biplane – the last of its class to serve with the RAF – was evolved as a private venture to meet Air Ministry Specification F.7/30. The prototype, known as the S.S.37, was flown for the first time in September 1934 and handed over to the RAF in April 1935 for evaluation with the serial number K 5200. With a Mercury IXS engine replacing the prototype's 645 hp Mercury VIS engine, and an enclosed cockpit, the fighter was placed in production, to Specification F.14/35, as the Gladiator Mk I. The initial contract was for twenty-three aircraft, delivery of which began to No 72 Squadron in February 1937. On 3 September 1939 the RAF had two hundred and ten Gladiator I's on charge, and two hundred and thirty-four Gladiator II's, the latter figure including thirty-eight Sea Gladiators. The Gladiator II differed from the Mk I in having an 840 hp Mercury VIIIA engine, desert equipment and other detail improvements; the Sea

Gladiators were interim conversions from RAF machines, fitted with catapult points and an arrester hook, and a fairing between the undercarriage legs for attaching a collapsible dinghy. A further sixty Sea Gladiators were subsequently built as such for the Fleet Air Arm, and ultimate production for the RAF amounted to four hundred and forty-eight. Gladiators were also exported widely before World War 2, to Belgium (twenty-two), China (thirty-six), Eire (four), Greece (two), Latvia (twenty-six), Lithuania (fourteen), Norway (twelve), Portugal (fifteen), South Africa (eleven) and Sweden (fifty-five). In addition, ex-RAF machines were supplied to Egypt (forty-five), Finland (thirty), Greece (twenty-three) and Iraq (fourteen), although several of these aircraft were later returned to the RAF. Production of Gladiators finally ended in 1940, and despite their obsolescence they still equipped thirteen RAF fighter squadrons at the outbreak of war. By the Battle of Britain in the late summer of 1940, only one UK fighter squadron was still flying Gladiators, and they had virtually disappeared from British service by mid-1941. They continued to serve in North Africa and on the Eastern Front for a time beyond this, but eventually ended their days on miscellaneous second-line duties, particularly on meteorological flights.

6 PZL P.11

The P.11, basically a more powerful derivative of the earlier P.7 designed by Ing Zygmunt Pulawski, was brought to fruition by his successor, Ing Wsiewolod Jakimiuk, after Pulawski's death in March 1931. The P.11/I, flown in September 1931, was the first of six prototypes, the sixth machine being representative of the initial production series of thirty P.11a fighters, which were powered by Skoda-built Mercury IVS2 engines. Delivery of these to Polish Air Force units began in 1934, and in the following year the Rumanian Air Force ordered fifty similar aircraft which, with slightly modified tail surfaces and Rumanian-built 595 hp Gnome-Rhône K.9 engines, were designated P.11b. The next Polish variant was the P.11c, placed in production in 1935, which featured a redesigned front fuselage with the engine and cockpit both repositioned to give the pilot a better view forward. This became the standard Polish version, one hundred and seventy-five P.11c's being built and incorporating increased armament (on some aircraft), redesigned tail surfaces and various equipment and other changes. Twelve Polish Air Force squadrons were equipped with P.11c's at the outbreak of World War 2, the P.11a's having meanwhile been withdrawn to training schools. During the seventeen days fighting that followed the Nazi invasion of Poland, one hundred and fourteen P.11c's were lost, though not before they had accounted for over one hundred and twenty *Luftwaffe* aircraft and carried out extensive strafing of the advancing *Wehrmacht*. Known familiarly as the *edenastka* (Eleventh), the P.11 was a versatile aeroplane, used for reconnaissance and liaison as well as for fighting, and its handling qualities made it popular with its pilots. It was, however, outclassed by its superior *Luftwaffe* opponents, although the Rumanian P.11's were also flown operationally during the Russo-German campaigns. Rumania remained the only non-Polish operator of the fighter, a Spanish order for fifteen having been frustrated in 1936. The proposed P.11d and P.11e export models did not materialise, but about eighty examples of the four-gun P.11f were built in Rumania in 1935-37. In July 1939 the PZL factories began production of the 4-gun P.11g, with a 840 hp Mercury VIII engine, but none had entered service before the invasion.

7 Chance Vought F4U Corsair
Originating with the Vought-Sikorsky Division of United Aircraft Corporation, the Vought V-166B prototype of the Corsair, designated XF4U-1, flew for the first time on 29 May 1940, becoming a few months later the first US warplane to fly faster than 400 mph (644 km/hr). This was the prelude to an 11-year production life, during which twelve thousand five hundred and seventy-one of these fighters were built, and a service career that lasted until the mid-1960s. The initial US Navy contract was for five hundred and eighty-four F4U-1's, delivery of which began in September 1942. Most of these went to Marine Corps or land-based Navy

squadrons, due to early difficulties in operating the Corsair from aircraft carriers, and the first operational missions were flown by Squadron VMF-124 of the USMC in February 1943. The Corsair's gull-wing configuration was devised to avoid the excessively long undercarriage legs that would otherwise have been necessary to provide clearance for the large-diameter propeller; but the far-aft cockpit position gave the pilot a poor view forward when landing. Hence from the six hundred and eighty-ninth F4U-1 onward, a new, raised cockpit hood was introduced on the Corsairs being built by Vought and by the Brewster and Goodyear factories. The Vought F4U-1C, otherwise similar, was armed with four 20 mm wing cannon instead of the former six machine-guns, while the F4U-1D (Goodyear FG-1D) had an R-2800-8W water-injection engine and provision for eight underwing rocket projectiles or two 1,000 lb (454 kg) bombs. The Brewster production line closed in 1944 after manufacturing seven hundred and thirty-five F3A-1 Corsairs; Goodyear ultimately built four thousand and fourteen FG-1's and -1D's and Vought four thousand six hundred and sixty-nine F4U-1's to -1D's. One thousand nine hundred and seventy-seven were supplied to the Fleet Air Arm as Corsair Mks I to IV, and a further four hundred and twenty-five to the RNZAF. The British Corsair Mks II to IV had each wing-tip clipped by 8 in (20·3 cm) to facilitate stowage aboard Royal Navy carriers, and preceded their

US counterparts into shipboard service, carrying out their first operational action in April 1944. In January 1943 Chance Vought became a separate division of UAC, and during that year twelve F4U-1's were modified to F4U-2's with four wing guns and radar in a fairing at the starboard wingtip. Others were converted to F4U-1P photo-reconnaissance aircraft. The next production model was the F4U-4 (Goodyear FG-4), with six 0·50 in guns in the wings and a 2,100 hp R-2800-1W engine. Delivery began toward the end of 1944, and despite cuts in orders at the end of the war, Chance Vought eventually completed two thousand three hundred and fifty-six F4U-4's and Goodyear two hundred FG-4's. These included batches of radar-equipped F4U-4E and -4N Corsairs for night fighting. Goodyear also built five F2G-1's and five F2G-2's, all with 3,000 hp R-4360-4 Wasp Major engines. During World War 2 the Corsairs in US service operated mostly from land bases in the Pacific theatre, where the distinctive note made by the airstream passing through their cooler inlets, allied to their eleven-to-one 'kill ratio' over their opponents, led the Japanese to refer to them by the grim but apt sobriquet 'Whistling Death'. Post-war production continued with the F4U-5 (which in its -5N version reached 470 mph = 756 km/hr), the AU-1 (originally F4U-6) and the F4U-7. These served with distinction in the Korean War and with the naval air arms of Argentina and France.

8 Grumman F4F Wildcat

Grumman's original proposals which won a 1936 US Navy development contract, were for a biplane carrier fighter based on its earlier successful biplane types. This design the XF4F-1, was then shelved in favour of a monoplane fighter whose prototype, the XF4F-2, was flown on 2 September 1937 powered by a 1,050 hp R-1830-66 Twin Wasp engine. The Navy decided to develop this still further, by ordering it to be rebuilt in a much-redesigned form as the XF4F-3, with an improved, supercharged XR-1830-76 engine This aircraft flew on 12 February 1939, and was followed six month later by an initial production order for the F4F-3. Eventually, two hundred and eighty-five F4F-3's were built. Deliveries to the US Navy late in 1940 were preceded by an order from France for one hundred G-36A fighters, the export designation of the F4F-3 when fitted with a 1,200 hp Wright R-1820-G205A engine. This order, later reduced to eighty-one, was diverted to Britain in mid-1940 after the fall of France, these aircraft and nine others being employed by the Fleet Air Arm under the title Martlet I. Thirty G-36A's, ordered by Greece were also diverted to Britain to become Martlet III's. Neither the F4F-3 nor the Martlet I embodied wing-folding, but this feature was incorporated in all but the first ten of an order for one hundred Martlet II (G-36B) fighters placed by Britain in 1940. (The other ten corresponded to the USN's sixty-five F4F-3A's, having non-folding wings nd R-1830-90 engines.) The US Navy's first folding-wing Wildcat was the Twin Wasp-engined F4F-4, Grumman building one thousand three hundred and eighty-nine, including two hundred and twenty F4F-4B's with Cyclone engines as Martlet IV's for the Fleet Air Arm. The Eastern Aircraft Division of General Motors delivered eight hundred and thirty-nine similar (but four-gunned) aircraft, designated FM-1, to the US Navy and three hundred and eleven to the FAA as Martlet V's. Eastern also built the FM-2, production version of Grumman's XF4F-8, with a 1,200 hp Wright R-1820-56 Cyclone engine and taller fin and rudder. Four thousand four hundred and seven went to the US Navy, and three hundred and seventy to Britain; the latter were designated Wildcat VI, the FAA having by now adopted the US name for the fighter. Grumman's final production version (twenty-one were built) was the F4F-7, a heavier and slower unarmed version, with fixed wings, extra fuel and photo-reconnaissance cameras.

) Grumman F6F Hellcat

The Hellcat, essentially a larger and more powerful development of the F4F Wildcat, flew in its original XF6F-1 form on 26 June 1942, with a 1,700 hp Wright R-2600-10 Cyclone engine. It was then re-engined with a 2,000 hp Pratt & Whitney R-2800-10 Double Wasp to become the XF6F-3, flying in this form on 30 July 1942. Production F6F-3's were virtually unchanged from this aircraft; they began to

appear early in October 1942, making their operational debuts with the British Fleet Air Arm in July 1943 and with the US Navy a month later. Production for the US Navy totalled four thousand six hundred and forty-six F6F-3's, including eighteen F6F-3E and two hundred and five F6F-3N night fighters; a further two hundred and fifty-two were supplied to the British Fleet Air Arm as the Hellcat I. Aerodynamic and control-surface improvements were introduced on the F6F-5, which entered production in 1944 and was able to operate in the fighter-bomber role with under-wing weapons. The F6F-5 was powered by an R-2800-10W engine capable of 2,200 hp using water-injection, and was both the principal and the last production Hellcat model. By November 1945, when production ended, twelve thousand two hundred and seventy-two Hellcats had been manufactured. Of these, six thousand four hundred and thirty-six were of the F6F-5 model, nearly one-fifth of which were F6F-5N night fighters; and nine hundred and thirty others were essentially similar Hellcat II's for the Royal Navy. Whereas its predecessor, the Wildcat, had been widely used in both the Atlantic and Pacific war areas, the Hellcat operated (with the USN and the FAA) predominantly in the Pacific; it was in service with land-based Marine Corps units as well as carrier-based squadrons, and was officially credited with nearly five thousand victims – some eighty per cent of all the enemy aircraft destroyed in air-to-air combat by USN carrier pilots during the war.

10 Republic P-47 Thunderbolt

A revised requirement, following the early air fighting in Europe, necessitated an almost complete redesign by Alexander Kartveli of the XP-47 light fighter projected early in 1939. This resulted in the XP-47B, which was almost twice as heavy and had a Double Wasp radial engine instead of the Allison in-line previously envisaged. Orders were placed in September 1940 for one hundred and seventy-one P-47B's and six hundred and two P-47C's, and on 6 May 1941 the XP-47B made its first flight. The B and C models were basically similar, but the C was given a slightly longer fuselage to improve manoeuvrability. The first Thunderbolts entered USAAF service in 1942, becoming operational with Eighth Air Force units over Europe in April 1943 and in the Pacific theatre some two months later. By this time, huge orders had been placed for the P-47D, which initially was but a refined version of the C. To this configuration, Republic factories manufactured five thousand four hundred and twenty-three P-47D's and Curtiss a further three hundred and fifty-four which were designated P-47G. A major design change was then introduced, on the P-47D-25 and subsequent batches, in which the cockpit view was vastly improved by cutting down the rear fuselage and fitting a 'teardrop' canopy. The weight thus saved also allowed extra fuel to be carried, but production batches from P-47D-27 onward required a dorsal fin fairing to offset the 'missing' keel area of the slimmer rear fuselage. Eight thousand one hundred and seventy-nine bubble-canopied P-47D's were completed at Farmingdale and Evansville, and this model served widely both as a fighter and fighter-bomber, especially with the USAAF in Europe. The RAF received two hundred and forty Thunderbolt I's (early P-47D) and five hundred and ninety Mk II's (later P-47D), while two hundred and three were allocated to the Soviet Air Force under Lend-Lease and eighty-eight to Brazil. The next production model (intervening suffix letters denoting various experimental machines) was the P-47M; this utilised the 2,800 hp R-2800-57 engine (with which the XP-47J had flown at 504 mph = 811 km/hr), allied to the P-47D airframe. It was an improvised version, produced hastily to counter the V1 flying-bomb attacks on Britain, and only one hundred and thirty were built. The last – and, at a maximum gross weight of 20,700 lb (9,390 kg), the heaviest – production Thunderbolt, was the P-47N, a very long-range escort and fighter-bomber variant of which Republic built one thousand eight hundred and sixteen Overall Thunderbolt production, which ended in December 1945, totalled fifteen thousand six hundred and sixty aircraft. About two-thirds of these survived the war, after which Thunderbolts found their way into numerous air forces; a few were still in service until the late 1960s.

11 Brewster F2A Buffalo

The F2A was the US Navy's first monoplane fighter, but so far as that service was concerned that was about its only distinction, and the aircraft's lack of favour is reflected in the small quantities that were built. Conversely, the export version in service with the Finnish Air Force was remarkably successful, the climate no doubt offsetting to some extent the overheating engines that were among the aircraft's early problems. Evolved as the Brewster Model 139, the prototype was completed to the designation XF2A-1 and flown for the first time in January 1938 with a 950 hp Wright Cyclone engine. In June fifty-four Model B-239's were ordered, as F2A-1's, with 940 hp R-1820-34 Cyclones. Eleven of these were delivered to the USN, nine of them joining Squadron VF-3 aboard the USS *Saratoga* from June 1939, and the remainder were released for export. These, plus one additional machine, were delivered to Finland (after reassembly by Saab in Sweden) by February 1940, and were fitted with four Browning machine-guns. They remained in front-line Finnish service until mid-1944. The US Navy, following flight trials of Brewster's XF2A-2 prototype (1,200 hp R-1820-40) in July 1939, ordered forty-three F2A-2's to replace the F2A-1's sent to Finland, and most of these followed the Finnish example by increasing the armament from two machine-guns to four. Foreign orders were received from Belgium (for the B-339) and the UK (B-339E). None of the former machines reached Belgium, but twenty-eight from that order were eventually delivered to the British Fleet Air Arm, and the RAF received one hundred and seventy as Buffalo I's. Rejected for European service, the Buffalo was allocated to RAF, RAAF and RNZAF squadrons in Malaya, but after the fall of Singapore the type was soon withdrawn from front-line British service. The Netherlands East Indies Army Air Corps received seventy-two B-339D's, which served from spring 1941 in that theatre, and ordered a further twenty B-439's which, although completed, were never delivered. The F2A-3, ordered meanwhile for the US Navy, introduced so many equipment and structural changes and additions that its much higher gross weight severely affected both its performance and its controllability, and only one hundred and eight were built before production ended in March 1942.

12 Nakajima Ki-27

The Ki-27 was one of three contenders for a 1935 JAAF single-seat fighter requirement, the others being the Kawasaki Ki-28 and the Mitsubishi Ki-18. The Nakajima design was selected for its lightness and manoeuvrability, although the Japanese Navy also selected the Mitsubishi A5M1, the carrier-based counterpart of the Ki-18, for production. Three Ki-27 prototypes were ordered by the JAAF, the first of which was flown on 15 October 1936; all three were powered by 650 hp Nakajima Ha-1a radial engines and differed only in having wings of three different areas. The largest-area wings became the standard type, and with these a pre-series batch of ten Ki-27's was completed in 1936–37. Series production began, with the Type 97 Model A, or Ki-27a, in the summer of 1937, this version being powered by the 710 hp Ha-1b model of the Nakajima engine. Units of the JAAF in Manchuria began to receive the first Ki-27a fighters in 1938, making their combat debut against the Soviet Air Force in the Siberian border disputes of 1938–39. Here they proved successful against the opposing I-15 biplane fighters, though less so against the monoplane I-16's. Nevertheless, in service with the JAAF and the Manchurian air force, they accounted for more than twelve hundred and fifty enemy fighters for the loss of only a hundred of their own number. The Ki-27a gave way in 1939 to the Ki-27b, which differed only in having a modified cockpit hood and detail improvements, and an eventual total of three thousand three hundred and eighty-six Ki-27's of the two versions were built. One thousand three hundred and seven of these were completed by the Tachikawa Aircraft Co and the Manchurian Aircraft Co. Although virtually obsolete by the time of Pearl Harbor, the Ki-27 was still in fairly widespread JAAF service, and was later allotted the Pacific code name 'Nate' by the Allies. It was encountered in Burma, China and Malaya during the first six months of the Pacific war, but after this was gradually withdrawn for conversion to a 2-seat advanced training role with a 450 hp engine and the new designation Ki-79. Three examples were completed of the Ki-27-Kai in 1940, but this improved model was abandoned with the new Ki-43 Hayabusa became available.

13 Mitsubishi A5M

Designed by Jiro Horikoshi, who later designed the famous Zero-Sen, the single-seat A5M was the JNAF's first monoplane fighter, produced to meet a naval requirement issued in 1934. It was an all-metal aeroplane, with a flush-riveted skin and – for the first time on a Japanese combat aircraft – full-scale landing flaps. During its maiden flight on 4 February 1935 the prototype showed an excellent turn of speed, and within days had flown 61 mph (98 km/hr) faster than its specification required. Powerplant was a 550 hp Nakajima Kotobuki 5 radial, and an inverted gull wing was utilised to improve the downward view from the cockpit. Due to problems encountered with this wing, and with the original engine, the second prototype had a 560 hp Kotobuki 3 and a conventional straight-tapered wing instead of the previous semi-elliptical shape. The powerplant continued to give trouble, several alternatives being tested before the choice of the 585 hp Kotobuki 2-Kai-1 was made to power the A5M1 Model 11 initial production model. Manufacture of the A5M1 – now as a carrier-based rather than a land-based fighter – began in 1936, and thirty-six of this model were completed. The A5M1 was then supplanted by the A5M2a Model 1, featuring wingtip 'wash-out', increased fin area and a 610 hp Kotobuki 2-Kai-3 engine. Mitsubishi A5M's formed part of the 2nd Combined Air Flotilla which embarked for Shanghai in September 1937, and carried out their first operational mission later that month. Flying both from carriers and from land bases, they proved remarkably successful against Soviet-built I-16's. The A5M2b Model 22 fighter-bomber proved less popular in service, its enclosed cockpit being heartily disliked by Japanese pilots. The A5M3a Model 23 was an experimental version fitted with a Hispano-Suiza *moteur-canon* engine. The final variants, the A5M4 Models 24 and 34, entered production in 1938 and were the principal JNAF versions at the time of Pearl Harbor. They were employed as first-line fighters only for the first six months of the Pacific war, then being withdrawn to serve as transition trainers for the A6M Zero-Sen; some aircraft were built from the outset as A5M4-K trainers. Pacific code-name for the A5M was 'Claude'. Seven hundred and eighty-two A5M's were built by Mitsubishi, and about two hundred by the Kyushu Aircraft Co.

4 Vultee BT-13 and BT-15 Valiant

The Valiant originated in the private-venture Model 51 prototype, produced in 1939 and powered by a 600 hp R-1340-45 Wasp engine. This was a 2-seat monoplane with a retractable undercarriage, and was accepted by the US Army in 1940 as the BC-3; it was the last aircraft to appear in the 'Basic Combat' category, which was then reclassified as AT (Advance Trainer). No production was undertaken of the Model 51, but substantial orders were placed in 1940 for the Vultee Model 54 basic trainer, under the designation BT-13. The Model 54 had essentially the same airframe as the Model 51, except for a slightly shorter fuselage occasioned by the use of the R-985-25 Wasp Junior engine, but its landing gear was non-retractable. Most of the USAAF's Valiants differed in minor details only, and the early contracts were, for their time, among the largest to be placed by the Army for any type of military aircraft. Three hundred examples were completed of the original BT-13, followed in 1941 by six thousand four hundred and seven BT-13A's (R-985-AN-1 engine) and one thousand one hundred and twenty-five BT-13B's (24-volt electrical system). One BT-13A was rebuilt by Vidal in 1942 with an all-plastic fuselage, being redesignated XBT-16, but no production was undertaken. Output of BT-13A airframes exceeded the available supplies of Wasp engines, and so in 1941 orders were also placed for one thousand six hundred and ninety-three examples of the BT-15, which was the designation of the BT-13A airframe fitted with a 450 hp Wright R-975-11 Whirlwind engine. The US Navy was also a large-scale user of Valiant trainers, receiving one thousand three hundred and fifty SNV-1's and six hundred and fifty SNV-2's corresponding respectively to the BT-13A and BT-13B. The Valiant did not remain long in US service after World War 2, but large numbers were sold abroad, notably in South America, where some were still in service in the early 1960s.

15 Blackburn Skua and Roc

When the Skua dive bomber entered service with the British Fleet Air Arm in November 1938 it was the first operational monoplane to be adopted by that service, and was also the first British combat aircraft designed specifically for the dive-bombing role. Two prototypes were ordered in 1935 to Specification O.27/34, and the first of these (K5178) was flown in 1937. Both were powered by 830 hp Bristol Mercury XII engines, but the similarly rated Perseus XII was chosen for the one hundred and ninety production aircraft ordered in July 1936. Delivery of these began in November 1938, the first recipient being No 800 Squadron aboard HMS *Ark Royal*. Two other squadrons were equipped with Skuas at the outbreak of World War 2, and one of No 803 Squadron's aircraft claimed the first *Luftwaffe* victim shot down in air combat on 25 September 1939, when it destroyed a Do 18 flying boat off the Norwegian coast. Carrying a 4-gun wing armament as well as a single rearward-firing gun, Skuas were employed as much as fighters as in their intended role, but their operational wartime career was comparatively brief, Fulmars and Sea Hurricane replacing them during 1941. In 193' a production order was placed for a fighter development of the Skua evolved to meet the requirements o Specification O.30/35. This aeroplane, the Blackburn Roc, followed the same tactical concept that produced the RAF's Defiant fighter and was similarly armed with four machine-guns in a power-operated dorsal turret. This necessitated a slightly wider fuselage than that o the Skua, and increased wing dihedral replaced the upturned wingtips that characterised the earlier design; otherwise the two aircraft were substantially alike. All one hundred and thirty-six Roc were built by Boulton Paul; the initial three acted as prototypes, the first of them (L 3057) flying on 23 December 1938. The third wa fitted experimentally with twin floats. However, the concept of the 2-seat rear-turreted fighter, devoid of any forward-firing armament was quickly proved unsound during the early fighting, and the Roc served only with two land-based squadrons of the FAA, between February 1940 and August 1941. I was then relegated to training or target towing duties, often with the turret removed.

16 Commonwealth Boomerang

Although only a 'stop-gap' fighter the Boomerang fulfilled an important role in the mid-war fighting in the Pacific theatre, more than making up in ruggedness, manoeuvrability and climb what it lacked in speed and range. At the time o earl Harbor the Royal Australian ir Force's fighter force consisted ly of two squadrons equipped ith American Buffalos, and in view the difficulty of obtaining rein-rcements quickly from the UK it as decided to produce an interim ghter locally. This was done by asing the new design on the ommonwealth Wirraway general-urpose aeroplane already in pro-uction in Australia, utilising as any of the latter's components as ossible. The resulting prototype, esignated CA-12 and serialled 46-1, flew on 29 May 1942 and was ut into production immediately terwards to meet an initial order r one hundred and five CA-12's laced in February 1942. These were llowed by ninety-five CA-13's and rty-nine CA-19's before production ased in January 1945, the later pes differing in minor details only. ne example was also completed the CA-14 (later CA-14A) oomerang, with a turbo-super-harged engine, but production of is version was rendered unneces-ry when the RAAF began to ceive supplies of high-altitude pitfires from the UK The first AAF unit to receive the Boomerang as No 2 OTU, in October 1942, nd the fighter made its operational ebut with No 84 Squadron in the lew Guinea battle area in April 943. It was also employed, latterly the ground-support role, in the orneo, Bougainville and New ritain areas as well as in Australia.

7   Polikarpov I-16

he I-16, known originally by the Central Design Bureau designation TsKB-12, was evolved by a Soviet team under the direction of Nikolai Polikarpov, and made its first flight on 31 December 1933. The proto-type was powered by a 450 hp M-22 (licence-built Bristol Jupiter) radial engine and was armed with two machine-guns. A second proto-type (TsKB-12*bis*), with a 725 hp M-25 (Wright Cyclone) engine, was flown on 18 February 1934. With a 480 hp M-22 engine, the original version (designated I-16 Type 1) entered squadron service during the second half of 1934, and it was a group of these which first appeared in public at the May Day fly-past over Moscow in 1935. Later in 1935 the Type 1 was joined in service by the Types 4 and 6, with M-25 and 730 hp M-25A engines respectively, and by a 2-seat trainer variant of the Types 4 and 10 known as the I-16UTI or UTI-4. Successively improved production batches in-cluded the Type 10 (750 hp M-25B engine, four machine-guns and open cockpit), Type 17 (with 20 mm cannon replacing the two wing guns), Types 18 and 24 (1,000 hp M-62), and the Type 24B with a 1,100 hp M-63 engine and enclosed cockpit. With the M-63 engine the I-16's maximum speed rose to 323 mph (520 km/hr). In its earlier forms, the I-16 was a reasonably fast and swift-climbing fighter for its time, and was the world's first low-wing single-seat monoplane fighter with retractable landing gear to enter service. The various power-plant and armament changes, how-ever, increased the gross weight and power loading of the Soviet fighter to the detriment of its rate of climb and airfield performance. The early I-16's saw service in Mongolia, and during the Spanish Civil War the Type 10 could out-manoeuvre the German Bf 109B in most respects. It could not, however, match the much-improved Bf 109E, despite the increases in speed brought about by the M-62 or M-63 engines. Nevertheless, the stocky little I-16 remained in Soviet Air Force service throughout the initial German onslaught, until the spring of 1943; during its World War 2 career it was conspicuously successful as a ground-attack aircraft, carrying rocket projectiles beneath the wings. The I-16, during its service life, received no official name, but a host of nicknames; of these, its native sobriquet of *Ishak* (little donkey) summarised as aptly as any the many tasks it was called upon to undertake. It is not widely appreciated that the I-16 was one of the most extensively built Soviet fighters: nearly five hundred were involved in the Spanish conflict, and estimates of total production suggest an overall figure not far short of twenty thousand aircraft.

18 **Macchi C.200 Saetta (Lightning)**

The Saetta was the first single-seat fighter designed for Aeronautica Macchi by Ing Mario Castoldi, and was evolved as part of the *Regia Aeronautica* re-equipment programme that followed the Italian campaigns in East Africa during the mid-1930s. Its neat contours were spoiled only by the bulky 850 hp

Fiat A.74 RC 38 radial engine that powered the first prototype (MM 336) on its first flight on 24 December 1937. During 1938, after completion of the second prototype, an initial production order was placed for ninety-nine Saettas, these having enclosed cockpits and a higher powered version of the A.74 engine. Delivery began in October 1939, and when Italy entered World War eight months later there were one hundred and fifty-six Saettas in service with the *Regia Aeronautica*. Their first operational appearance of the war was over Malta and Saettas subsequently served in Greece, North Africa, Russia, Yugoslavia and wherever the Italian forces were engaged. A total of three hundred and ninety-seven C.200's were built by Macchi, in addition to which Breda completed approximately five hundred and SAI-Ambrosini about three hundred. Most of the wartime production aircraft reverted to open cockpits, which were much preferred by Italian pilots. Although not fast or well-armed by contemporary standards, the Saetta was a well-built and extremely manoeuvrable fighter, capable of withstanding considerable battle damage or climatic extremes. Toward the end of its career it was employed on escort or fighter-bomber duties, in the latter role carrying eight small or two larger bombs beneath the wings. In 1938 appeared the prototype Macchi C.201, with fuselage redesigned to take a 1,000 hp Fiat A.76 RC 40 radial, and in 1941 one C.200 was refitted with a Piaggio

.XIX engine, but neither of these experiments reached production status, being discarded in favour of the much more promising C.202 powered by the Daimler-Benz inverted-Vee engine. The C.202 is described separately.

9   Fiat G.50 Freccia (Arrow)

The G.50, designed by Ing Giuseppe Gabrielli, was one of six designs (another being the Macchi C.200) submitted to the Italian Air Ministry in 1936 for an all-metal, single-seat fighter monoplane with retractable landing gear. The first prototype (MM 334) was flown on 26 February 1937, powered by an 840 hp Fiat A.74 RC 38 radial engine. An initial order for forty-five G.50's was given to the Fiat subsidiary CMASA, at Marina di Pisa, and delivery of these began in January 1938. Twelve of this batch were sent immediately to Spain to join the Italian *Aviazione Legionaria* fighting with the Republican forces under General Franco. Their participation was too short for a conclusive evaluation of the G.50's combat worth, but it was decided to maintain production as an insurance against possible difficulties in production of the Macchi C.200. A further two hundred G.50's were ordered, and a total of one hundred and eighteen G.50's were on *Regia Aeronautica* strength when Italy entered World War 2 in June 1940. Late in 1939 the Finnish government ordered thirty-five, most of which were delivered by the spring of 1940, and these gave excellent service until May 1944 before being withdrawn.

With the *Regia Aeronautica* the Freccia served in interceptor, ground-attack, convoy and bomber escort roles, and was employed in Belgium, Greece and the Balkan theatre as well as in the Mediterranean and North Africa during the first half of the war. Two hundred and forty-five examples of the original G.50 were built by Fiat-CMASA before this version was supplanted in production by the improved G.50*bis*, whose prototype was flown on 9 September 1940. This model had a refined fuselage design, modified canopy, a shorter and broader rudder, and increased fuel tankage and protective armour. Fiat's CMASA and Turin factories completed four hundred and twenty-one of this version. CMASA also designed and built one hundred and eight G.50B tandem 2-seat unarmed trainer models. Nine G.50*bis* were delivered to the Croatian Air Force. Experimental variants tested included the DB 601-engined G.50V of 1941, discarded in favour of the G.55 design, and the G.50*bis*-A, an enlarged 2-seat fighter-bomber with increased armament and bomb load, flown in 1942 but abandoned after the Italian Armistice. The proposed G.50*ter* was rendered abortive when the A.76 engine intended for it was abandoned before the aircraft's first flight in July 1941.

20   FFVS J 22

Before and immediately after the outbreak of World War 2, the *Flygvapnet* (Royal Swedish Air Force) had to face the prospect that orders placed abroad for combat aircraft either could not be fulfilled at all, because of the demands of war, or could be placed only for lesser types which would be no improvement over those already in service. With its major aircraft constructor, the Saab company, fully committed to production of bombers and reconnaissance aircraft, the *Flygvapnet* lacked any immediate prospect of an efficient, modern single-seat fighter available in sufficient quantity. Thus, in the autumn of 1940, the Royal Swedish Air Board set up a team, with Bo Lundberg as chief designer, to produce a stop-gap fighter, using wood and steel in its construction to conserve supplies of light alloys for more urgent needs. Design work began in January 1941, and on 1 September 1942 the prototype fighter made its first flight. It was powered by a Swedish-built 1,065 hp Pratt & Whitney Twin Wasp radial engine, and bore a superficial resemblance to the German Fw 190. An initial batch of sixty fighters, designated J 22, had been ordered in March 1942, and component manufacture was distributed among some five hundred companies – most of them outside the aviation industry. Assembly and flight testing of the completed aircraft was undertaken by the Flygförvaltningens Verkstad (FFVS) at Bromma, near Stockholm, which was ultimately responsible for one hundred and eighty J 22's. The *Flygvapnet*'s own workshop at Arboga completed a further eighteen. The first J 22 was completed in September 1943, and deliveries began two months later to

F9 Wing at Gothenburg. Th fighter was produced in J 22A an J 22B versions: the former with tw 13·2 mm M/39A and two 7·9 mm M/22F machine-guns and the latte with all four guns of the M/39A type. Some J 22's were still ii service in 1952, although the typ had by then been largely replace by the Saab-21R jet fighter.

21 Focke-Wulf Fw 190

The Fw 190, indissolubly associate with the name of its designer Dipl-Ing Kurt Tank, was technical ly one of the most advanced, an operationally one of the mos eminent, fighters and fighter bombers of 1939–45. One of two designs submitted by Focke-Wulf ii response to an RLM specification c 1937, the prototype Fw 190V (D-OPZE) first flew on 1 June 1939 powered by a 1,550 hp BMW 13 radial engine. The second prototyp was similarly powered, but in sub sequent aircraft the larger an heavier 1,600 hp BMW 801 wa substituted. Eighteen pre-produc tion Fw 190A-0's were ordere in 1940, most of them having 3 ft 3½ in (1·00 m) increase in wing span that became standard on pro duction aircraft. These began wit one hundred Fw 190A-1's, deliver of which started late in 1940, an continued with A-2 and A-3 sub types with improved armament This was increased to six guns in the Fw 190A-3, powered by a 1,700 hp BMW 801Dg engine. Early opera tional use was made of the Fw 19 in the low-altitude hit-and-ru raids over southern England durin

941–42, and by the end of the latter year nearly two thousand of these fighters had been built. New variants included the A-4 (BMW 801D-2, giving 2,100 hp with power boost), the A-4/U8 (reduced gun armament but carrying drop-tanks and a 1,102 lb = 500 kg bomb load), and the rocket-carrying A-4/R6. By the end of 1942 the Fw 190 was also in widespread service in North Africa and on the Russian Front, in even greater numbers than in Europe. The Fw 190A-5 was produced primarily for night fighting and close-support duties; the A-6 and A-7 featured further improvements in firepower; the A-8, A-9 and A-10 were mostly fighter-bombers, with different versions of the BMW 801 engine, although some were utilised as all-weather fighters and others converted to tandem-seat trainers. A small number of Fw 190B and C prototypes were completed, with supercharged DB 603 inverted-Vee engines, but both models were discarded in favour of the long-nosed Fw 190D. This model evolved from tests with a few prototype aircraft fitted with the 1,776 hp Junkers Jumo 213A-1 engine, a liquid-cooled unit whose annular radiator duct presented a radial-engined appearance. The initial Fw 190D-0 and D-1 aircraft were delivered for evaluation in the spring and summer of 1943, and were characterised by their longer, newly contoured engine cowlings, lengthened rear fuselage and (on the D-1) increased fin area. The first major production D model was the Fw 190D-9, which entered service with JG.3 in 1943.

This was an interceptor; subsequent versions, equipped for ground-attack, included the D-11 (two wing-mounted 30 mm MK 108 cannon), and the 2,060 hp Jumo 213F-engined D-12 and D-13 (single nose-mounted MK 108 or MK 103 respectively). Following the Fw 190D on the production line came another fighter-bomber, the Fw 190G. On this, the fixed armament was reduced to permit a single 3,968 lb (1,800 kg) bomb or its equivalent in smaller weapons to be carried externally. The Fw 190F, out of sequence, followed the G model into production. Both models were powered by the BMW 801D radial engine, but the Fw 190F had additional provision for twenty-four underwing rocket projectiles or a 3,086 lb (1,400 kg) armour-piercing bomb beneath the fuselage. Total Fw 190 production, excluding prototypes, amounted to twenty thousand and fifty-one machines, over six and a half thousand of which were fighter-bomber variants. The long-span, DB 603-engined Ta 152 developed by Dr Tank from the Fw 190D, succeeded it in production, but was in service only in comparatively small numbers when the war ended.

22 IVL Myrsky (Storm)

Finland's only nationally designed combat aircraft during World War 2 was the Myrsky, designed by Dr E. Wegelius and built by the Industria Valtion Lentokonetehdas (Finnish State Aircraft Factory) at Tampere. Like Sweden's J 22 fighter, the Myrsky was powered by the

Swedish-built Twin Wasp radial engine, and was flown for the first time in 1942. The first two aircraft (MY-1 and MY-2) acted as prototypes, but both of these and the first two production Myrsky I's were lost in a series of accidents which revealed numerous latent defects in the fighter's design and construction. The aircraft was unstable longitudinally; its landing gear was insufficiently strong, and so were the wing-root attachments; and the laminated plywood outer skin of the wings could not withstand the stresses of combat manoeuvres. A completely redesigned wing, strengthened undercarriage and other essential modifications were introduced from the fifth aircraft onward, and in 1944 forty-seven aircraft were completed in this form with the designation Myrsky II. Even with these improvements, the fighter was slow and poorly armed by contemporary standards; it was not popular with its pilots, and was used only in a limited role against the German forces during their withdrawal from Finland. Ten further aircraft, designated Myrsky III, had been partially completed before their production was halted by the Allied Control Commission late in 1944.

23 Bloch 151, 152 and 155

The Bloch 150–01 prototype which preceded this line of French single-seat fighters could scarcely have had a less auspicious start to its career, for twice, in July and August 1936, it failed to leave the ground during attempts to make its first flight. This was eventually accomplished, after much structural redesign and the substitution of a more efficient Gnome-Rhône engine, on 2 September 1937. Following ye further redesign, to make the aircraft suitable for mass production, it was ordered as the Bloch 151; but, instead of more than two hundred of these fighters scheduled for deliver to the *Armée de l'Air* by 1 April 1939 only one had actually been delivered by that date, and the type's disappointing performance, coupled with engine overheating and control problems, led to its relegation to a training role after modifications had been carried out. Only one hundred and forty Bloch 151's were completed. In April 1938 a contract had been placed for three more prototype aircraft, which emerged as the Bloch 152, 153 and 154, but only the 152 achieved production status. The Bloch 152-01, differing chiefly from its predecessor in having a 1,030 hp Gnome-Rhône 14N-21 engine, first flew on 15 December 1938. Production of the Bloch fighters was shared by the factories of the SNCA du Sud-Ouest, which by now had absorbed the Marcel Bloch company; initial orders for the Bloch 152 totalled two hundred and eighty eight, but only one squadron was equipped with the type at the outbreak of war, and its 152's were non operational. By January 1940 the *Armée de l'Air* had just over a hundred Bloch 152's in flyable condition with nearly twice that number non operational from lack of propellers An eventual total of four hundred and eighty-two were taken on harge, only about two-thirds of which remained by the end of July 940. Many of the survivors were used by the Vichy Air Force, and twenty were allocated by Germany to the Rumanian Air Force. At about the same time, the Royal Hellenic Air Force received nine Bloch 151's (of twenty-five ordered) from France. The Bloch 155 was a development of the 152 with a ,180 hp Gnome-Rhône 14N-49 engine, flown for the first time on 3 December 1939. Production of this version began, but only nine had been accepted by the *Armée de l'Air* before the fall of France. Others were used by the Vichy forces until seized by the German authorities in 942. The final development, the Bloch 157, promised to be far superior to its predecessors in every respect, but its evolution was forestalled by the German occupation of France. However, completion of the prototype was authorised, and this flew in March 1942, subsequently reaching a level speed of 441 mph (710 km/hr).

24 Fokker D.XXI

The Fokker D.XXI was designed in 1935 by E. Schatzki, initially for the Royal Netherlands East Indies Army Air Service. The prototype (FD-322), powered by a 645 hp Bristol Mercury VIS engine, made its first flight on 27 March 1936. The first contract was not placed until the early summer of 1937, when thirty-six of these fighters, powered by 830 hp Mercury VII or VIII engines, were ordered instead for the home air force. Delivery began in 1938, the prototype also being brought up to production standard and placed in service. Twenty-nine serviceable D.XXI's were available when Holland was invaded on 10 May 1940, divided between the 1st, 2nd and 5th Fighter Groups of the LVA at De Kooy, Schiphol and Ypenburg. After three day's fighting even these had to be grounded due to lack of ammunition, but in that short period they gave a good account of themselves against the faster and better-equipped *Luftwaffe* fighters, thanks to good handling qualities and a high degree of manoeuvrability. In 1937 seven Dutch-built D.XXI's were supplied to Finland, where the IVL (State Aircraft Factory) at Tampere built a further thirty-eight under licence for the 2nd Air Regiment of the Finnish Air Force during 1938. Finnish production of the D.XXI was then suspended until 1941, the Mercury VIII engines being more urgently needed for the Blenheim bombers being manufactured in the country. In 1940, however, a quantity of 825 hp Twin Wasp Junior engines was purchased from the USA, and the IVL produced fifty Wasp-powered D.XXI's in 1941 and a final five in 1944. These fought with distinction in the Russo-Finnish winter war of 1939–40 and in later campaigns, frequently with ski landing gear. A few were licence-built in Spain, before the Carmoli factory fell into Nationalist hands during the Civil War. In July 1937 two Dutch-built D.XXI's were bought by the Danish government, whose Naval Dockyard at Kløvermarken built ten more in 1939–40. These were serving with the Royal Danish Air Force's 2nd Eskadrille at Vaerløse when Denmark was invaded in April 1940. Contrary to popular belief, only one Danish-built D.XXI was fitted, experimentally, with 20 mm Madsen cannon in underwing blisters; standard armament of the remainder was two 8 mm DISA machine-guns in the upper front fuselage. Danish machines were also powered by the Mercury VIII engine, and not the Mercury VIS, as frequently stated.

25 Mitsubishi A6M Zero-Sen

The exacting terms of the 12-*Shi* (1937) JNAF specification to which Jiro Horikoshi designed the celebrated Zero fighter resulted in the most widespread service career ever enjoyed by a Japanese combat aircraft. Two A6M1 prototypes were built, each with a 780 hp Zuisei 13 radial engine, and the first flight was made on 1 April 1939. Production began in 1940 with the A6M2 Model 11, the only major change being the adoption of the more powerful Sakae 12 engine. Following operational evaluation of fifteen Zeros in China, the JNAF officially accepted the type at the end of July 1940. Sixty-four Model 11's were completed, the Model 21 with folding wingtips following these into production in November 1940. This was the major JNAF version at the time of Pearl Harbor, although in mid-1941 the A6M3 Model 32 made its first appearance. Similar at first to the A6M2, except for its 1,300 hp supercharged Sakae 21 engine, the

A6M3's performance was later improved by removing the foldable tip section of each wing. This, however, reduced the Zero's manoeuvrability and the full-span wing, in non-folding form, was restored in the A6M3 Model 22. In the air fighting over Guadalcanal early in 1943 it began to be apparent that the Zero was no longer maintaining its early superiority over its Allied opponents. Hence the A6M5 Model 52 was developed, retaining the Sakae 21 engine but having a shorter-span wing which was, in essence, that of the Model 32 with the square tips rounded off. Sub-types produced included the A6M5a Model 52A (strengthened wings and increased ammunition), A6M5b Model 52B (increased armament and armour protection), and A6M5c Model 52C (further protective armour, two 20 mm and three 13 mm guns), all of which appeared in 1944. The Model 52C was produced primarily to offset the non-availability of Mitsubishi's new A7M1 carrier fighter, but its higher gross weight had such a penalising effect upon performance that comparatively few were built. The A6M6c Model 53C had a Sakae 31 engine with methanol injection, bullet-proof fuel tanks and underwing rocket rails. When supplies of Sakae engines were compromised by continued Allied air attacks, there appeared the A6M8c Model 54C with a 1,500 hp Mitsubishi Kinsei 62 and armed only with four wing guns. In 1945 Mitsubishi built four hundred and sixty-five examples of a special *Kamikaze* version, the A6M7 Model 63, and several hundred more

Zeros of all versions were also expended in suicide attacks. A total of ten thousand nine hundred and thirty-seven Zeros of all versions was built by VJ-day. Mitsubishi built three thousand eight hundred and seventy-nine of these, but the principal manufacturer was Naka-jima, whose factories produced six thousand two hundred and seven-teen landplane Zeros and three hundred and twenty-seven examples of a twin-float version designated A6M2-N. In addition, five hundred and eight A6M2-K 2-seat conversion trainers were built by Hitachi and Sasebo Naval Air Arsenal, and six A6M5-K's by Hitachi and Omura Naval Arsenal.

26 Reggiane Re 2000 Falco I (Falcon)

Reggiane SA, a Caproni subsidiary, produced during the late 1930's a series of compact single-seat fighters whose merits were greater than their production or extent of service might suggest. The line began with the Re 2000, designed in 1938 by Ings Antonio Alessio and Roberto Longhi, whose prototype (MM 408) first flew on 24 May 1939. It could out-manoeuvre both the Macchi C.200 and the Messerschmitt Bf 109E, against which it was flown in comparative trials, but its less robust construction led the *Regia Aeronautica* to cancel its original intent to order two hundred production machines. The Re 2000 met with greater suc-cess in the export market, however, which accounted for most of the one hundred and seventy that were eventually built. Sixty, ordered by

Sweden in 1940, served as the J 20 with the *Flygvapnet* from 1941 to 1945; while seventy more were delivered to the Hungarian Air Force, in 1940–41. In addition, the MAVAG company in Hungary built a further one hundred and ninety-two under licence, most of them with locally built Gnome-Rhône 14K engines and Gebauer machine-guns. The Hungarian Re 2000 was known as the *Héja*, and was employed chiefly on the Russian Front. Other prospective customers whose intentions were forestalled by the war included Finland, Spain, Switzerland, the UK and Yugo-slavia. Some twenty-eight Re 2000's, taken out of the export lines, were evaluated by the Italian govern-ment, as a result of which ten air-craft were 'navalised' in 1940–41 to serve with the *Regia Marina* as catapult fighters aboard Italian war-ships; but these saw no operational service. Meanwhile a strengthened prototype (MM 454) with 1,175 hp Piaggio P.XIX RC 45 engine, pro-duced originally to overcome the Italian Air Ministry's reservations about the Re 2000's structural weak-nesses, became instead the prototype for the Re 2002 *Ariete* (Ram) fighter-bomber and ground attack aircraft. Less than fifty Re 2002's were built, but these did enter service, in 1942, with the *Regia Aeronautica*. Armed with two 12·7 mm and two 7·7 mm guns, the *Ariete* could carry a useful load of up to 1,433 lb (650 kg) of bombs, and was also tested as a torpedo carrier. It took part in the defence of Sicily during the Allied landings. The basic Re 2000 airframe was also utilised in the development of two variants powered by Daimler-Benz liquid-cooled inverted-Vee engines: the Re 2001 *Falco* II and the Re 2005 *Sagittario* (Archer).

27 Lavochkin La-5 and La-7

The La-5 came into being early in 1942 primarily as a developed version of the LaGG-3 single-seat fighter which had entered service a year or so earlier. Although following a substantially similar structural layout, the prototype La-5 featured improved armament and an all-round-vision cockpit canopy, and was powered by a 1,330 hp Shvetsov M-82F radial engine. Following successful completion of its flight trials programme, the La-5 entered production in mid-summer 1942 and was in service by the autumn. Early combat encounters showed it to be a better all-round performer than the Bf 109G which was its most formidable opponent, although the La-5's climb rate was inferior to the German fighter. Attempts to improve this aspect of the Soviet fighter's performance resulted in 1943 in the La-5FN, a reduced-weight version with a 1,510 hp M-82FN direct-injection engine, which exhibited greater climbing power and manoeuvrability than either the Bf 109G or the Fw 190A-4. Its flying qualities were reportedly excellent, and the La-5FN proved as popular as it was efficient. A 2-seat trainer version, the La-5UTI, was also produced in quantity. The La-7, similarly powered to the La-5FN, featured a revised engine cowling

and other aerodynamic refinements, and improved further upon its predecessor's combat performance at some cost in fuel load and range. This type entered Soviet Air Force service in mid-1944, production being maintained in parallel with that of the La-5FN. The basic design was taken a stage further in the La-9, with redesigned wingtips, tail surfaces and cockpit, and a 1,850 hp ASh-82FNV engine. Although this began to enter service late in 1944, it saw little or no war-time action, but remained to become a standard post-war fighter with Soviet bloc air forces. The line ended with the La-11, first evolved in 1945 as a long-range escort development of the La-9 and later used in the Korean War of 1950–53. Operating as low-altitude fighters, fighter-bombers and ground-attack aircraft, the La-5 and La-7 had few, if any, equals on the Eastern Front. Both types also served with a Czechoslovak Air Division of the Soviet forces during 1944–45. No precise account of overall production is available, but the total built is thought to have been between fifteen and twenty thousand.

28 Nakajima Ki-43 Hayabusa (Peregrine Falcon)

The Ki-43 was designed by Dr Hideo Itokawa in 1938 as a potential replacement for the JAAF's Ki-27 fighter, and the first of three prototypes was flown early in January 1939. Despite excellent speed and range qualities, the aircraft was somewhat heavy on the controls, and the first of the ten pre-production aircraft, which appeared in November 1939, was a lighter aeroplane with increased wing area and 'combat flaps' that vastly improved its handling characteristics. It was quickly ordered in quantity and was to remain in production throughout the Pacific war, by which time five thousand seven hundred and fifty-one had been delivered. The initial version, the Ki-43-Ia Model 1A, entered production in March 1941. Fire-power was improved in later versions, the major early version being the Ki-43-Ic Model 1C with two fuselage-mounted 12·7 mm guns. At the time of Pearl Harbor about forty Ki-43's were in JAAF service and, although extremely popular as flying machines, combat experience soon revealed a need for greater armour protection and increased engine power. These appeared in the Ki-43-IIa Model 2A, built by Tachikawa factories in 1942–43, which was powered by the 1,105 hp Sakae Ha-115 engine and could carry two 551 lb (250 kg) underwing bombs. This was succeeded in November 1943 by the Ki-43-IIb Model 2B, a clipped-wing variant of the Model 2A with greater manoeuvrability. Joint production by Nakajima and Tachikawa from December 1944 yielded the Ki-43-IIIa Model 3A (1,250 hp Kasei Ha-112 engine), the last production version. Two prototypes were completed of the Tachikawa-developed Model 3B, with two 20 mm cannon, but no production was achieved before VJ-day. The Hayabusa was encountered in particularly strong numbers during the battle for Leyte Island, and in the defence of the Kurile Islands north of Japan, but it served widely throughout all the mainland and island battle areas of south-east Asia, in suicide attacks during 1944–45, and in the final defence of the Japanese homeland. The Hayabusa (Pacific code name 'Oscar') was an excellent and versatile fighter, its only serious drawback being its lack of adequate armament.

29 Nakajima Ki-44 Shoki (Demon)

The Ki-44, a contemporary of the Nakajima Ki-43, was designed in response to a 1938 JAAF requirement for a short-range interceptor capable of defending Japanese home targets. The first of ten prototypes was flown in August 1940, and some aircraft from this batch were placed temporarily in operational service during the early part of the Pacific war. The 4-gunned *Shoki* proved to be a fast-climbing and highly manoeuvrable fighter, but its bulk and high take-off and landing speeds created an initial resistance to its introduction among JAAF pilots. Once its different handling requirements were mastered, however, the Ki-44 became more readily accepted for the effective fighter that it undoubtedly was. Production began with forty Ki-44-Ia Model 1A's, delivery of which began in the summer of 1942. The Model 1A was powered by a Nakajima Ha-41 engine, but the five subsequent production versions all had the 1,450 hp Nakajima Ha-109. The Ki-44-Ib and -Ic (Models 1B and 1C), which entered service in 1943, each had four 12·7 mm guns, as did the Ki-44-IIb Model 2B; the Ki-44-IIc Model 2C had a pair of 40 mm cannon replacing the wing guns; while the lighter-weight Ki-44-III Model 3 had these replaced in turn by 20 mm weapons. Comparatively few Model 3's were completed, but the *Shoki* Model 2C performed particularly well against high-flying formations of US Liberator bombers. Codenamed 'Tojo' by the Allies, the *Shoki* operated chiefly over its native terrain, although small numbers were encountered in Burma and New Guinea during the later war years. A total of one thousand two hundred and thirty-three, in all versions, were manufactured.

30 Nakajima Ki-84 Hayate (Gale)

Despite a superficial likeness to the Ki-43 and Ki-44 fighters, the Ki-84 Hayate was an entirely new single-seater, designed under the direction of T. Koyama from April 1942 to succeed its stablemates in service. Greater attention was given, following combat experience in earlier fighters, to such features as armour protection and self-sealing fuel tanks, and the Ki-84 was also more sturdily built than its forebears. But for a series of difficulties encountered with its Homare powerplant, much more would doubtless have been heard of the Hayate in the Pacific air fighting, for it could match most of the best US fighters at heights of up to 30,000 ft (9,000 m). The first of two Ki-84 prototypes was flown in April 1943, and these two aircraft were soon followed by an initial

batch of eighty-three for service evaluation. Delivery of production aircraft to the JAAF started in April 1944, and the fighter (code-named 'Frank' by the Allies) was first met in action five months later, operating from Chinese bases near Hangkow. All three variants of the Ki-84-I were similarly powered, differing chiefly in the armament installed. The Model 1A had 12·7 mm nose and 20 mm wing guns; in the Model 1B all four were of 20 mm calibre; while in the Model 1C the wing guns were 30 mm calibre. The Hayate was employed as a day and night fighter, dive bomber and ground-attack aircraft, but was hampered operationally by faults in the insufficiently developed Homare engine, which restricted its performance capabilities above 30,000 ft, and to some weakness in the main landing gear. The latter created several attempts to evolve a lighter-weight version of the Hayate, most of which eventually proved to be heavier than the original! They included the all-wood Ki-106, the mainly steel-built Ki-113 and the mixed construction Ki-84-II. Projects incomplete when the war ended included the supercharged Ki-84-III and Ki-84R, and the Ki-84P with increased wing area and 2,500 hp Ha-219 engine. Most promising of all was the Ki-114, developed by Mansyu and tested briefly before VJ-day. This had a Ha-112-II engine, yet in spite of increased length and enlarged tail surfaces was some ten per cent lighter than the Ki-84-Ia. Total number of Hayates delivered to the JAAF was three thousand four hunred and seventy: Mansyu Hikoki built about a hundred, but most were manufactured at Nakajima's Ota and Utsonomiya factories.

31 Mitsubishi J2M Raiden (Thunderbolt)

The Raiden was the first JNAF aircraft designed specifically for interception, regarded prior to 1938 strictly as a function of the Army Air Force. Proposals were submitted in April 1940, and the first of three J2M1 prototypes was flown on 20 March 1942, powered by a 1,430 hp Kasei 13 radial engine. Tests revealed that performance was below specification, the landing gear retraction mechanism unreliable, the engine far from satisfactory and the cockpit view, particularly during landing, extremely poor. A deeper cockpit hood, 1,820 hp Kasei 23a engine and other improvements were incorporated from the fourth machine, and this – designated J2M2 Model 11 – was eventually accepted for production in October 1942. One hundred and fifty-nine Model 11's were built, entering service in December 1943 despite continuing engine troubles and the breaking up of several aircraft while on test. The next and most widely used models two hundred and eighty-one built by Mitsubishi) were the J2M3 and J2M3a Models 21 and 21A. One of the latter was given an even deeper cockpit hood in mid-1944, being redesignated J2M6a Model 31A. In May 1944 the first example was completed of the J2M5 Model 33, with a 1,820 hp Kasei 26a and the wing armament reduced to two 20 mm cannon. This version proved to be one of the best high-altitude Japanese interceptors of the war, and post-war US test reports spoke of its 'splendid climbing performance' and 'fine controllability'. The design was now vindicated, but supply shortages of the Kasei 26a engine which was the key to its success prevented more than thirty-five J2M5's being completed, and proposals to re-engine the J2M3 and J2M3a with this unit had to be forsaken. Two J2M4's were built to study the possible advantages of fitting engine turbo-superchargers, but this project was abandoned. The Raiden (Allied code name 'Jack') was used almost exclusively for home defence, but was also encountered in the Marianas campaign in September 1944.

32 Kawanishi N1K Shiden (Violet Lightning)

The Shiden was unique among World War 2's landplane fighters in being evolved from a floatplane fighter, the N1K1 Kyofu (Mighty Wind). The result proved, in the end, to be among the finest fighter aircraft to operate in the Pacific theatre. Adaptation of the original Kyofu design by Dr Kikuhara had already begun in April 1942, four months before the floatplane's first flight, and the first landplane N1K1-J made its maiden flight on 24 July 1943. A problem was created by the 1,990 hp Homare 21 engine, which required a large-diameter propeller and hence (because of the mid-wing configuration) an unusually stalky main landing gear, with associated problems of retraction. The Homare in any case was a troublesome engine, pressed into production without sufficient development, and production of the Model 11 Shiden, which began in August 1943, was thus subject to constant interruption for modifications found necessary as the flight trials progressed. A second N1K1-J production line was established, but in the meantime a major redesign had been initiated in the autumn of 1943, aimed at simplifying production. The redesigned fighter, known as the N1K2-J Model 21 Shiden-Kai, required only about two-thirds of the airframe parts of its predecessor, and by adopting a low-wing configuration successfully overcame the landing gear retraction problem as well. Aerodynamic refinements included a slightly longer fuselage and redesigned vertical tail surfaces, but the problematical Homare powerplant was retained. The first N1K2-J flew on 3 April 1944, and by the middle of the year the Shiden-Kai had entered production. Inevitably, output continued to be hampered by modifications, as well as by Allied air attacks on the factories concerned. Thus, compared with one thousand and eleven N1K1-J's built (including prototypes), only four hundred and six N1K2-J's were completed by Kawanishi. To the latter were added a further twenty-three completed in small quantities by the Aichi, Mitsubishi and Showa companies and by the Naval Air Arsenals at Hiro and Omura. Several versions, with alternative engines or increased armament, were tested or projected before the war ended, but none reached production status. Both operational models of the Shiden received the Allied code name 'George', and were prominent in the Philippines, around Formosa and over the Japanese island of Honshu among other Pacific battle areas.

33 North American AT-6 Texan

The original NA-16 design, which ultimately gave rise to one of the most famous training aeroplanes ever built, was entered in modified form, as the NA-26, in a USAAC competition of March 1937 for an aircraft in what was then known as the 'Basic Combat' category. One hundred and eighty similar aircraft were eventually ordered by the US Army as BC-1's, and a further four hundred produced for the RAF as the Harvard I. Sixteen of an improved model for the US Navy were designated SNJ-1. North American built ninety-two BC-1A's and three BC-2's, but the new 'Advance Trainer' classification then replaced the former BC category, and nine of the BC-1A's were delivered under the trainer's new designation AT-6, being followed by a further eighty-five aircraft ordered as AT-6's. The BC-1A/AT-6 differed from the original BC-1/Harvard I primarily in its squared-off wingtips and new straight-edged rudder, which remained the standard appearance of the Texan/Harvard throughout the rest of its considerable production life. Purchases and Lend-Lease supplies of the AT-6 to the RAF (as the Harvard II) totalled one thousand one hundred and seventy-three, the majority being used at EATS airfields in Canada. The US Navy's sixty-one SNJ-2's resembled the SNJ-1, except for an engine change and detail differences. The next large-scale model was the NA-77, one thousand five hundred and forty-nine being built as AT-6A's for the US Army and two hundred and seventy as SNJ-3's for the Navy. Four hundred AT-6B's for the USAAF were basically similar, but were specially equipped for gunnery training and utilised the R-1340-AN-1 Wasp engine in place of the AT-6A's R-1340-49. The former engine became standard for all subsequent Texans, the next basic model of which was the NA-88. This was built with a 12-volt electrical system (two thousand nine hundred and seventy AT-6C's and two thousand four hundred SNJ-4's) and with a 24-volt system (three thousand seven hundred and thirteen AT-6D's and one thousand three hundred and fifty-seven SNJ-5's). Seven hundred and twenty-six AT-6C's were supplied to the RAF as the Harvard IIA; the RAF received three hundred and fifty-one AT-6D's, and the Fleet Air Arm five hundred and sixty-four, as the Harvard III. Final American-built model was the NA-121, twenty-five of which became the USAAF's AT-6F and nine hundred and thirty-one the USN's SNJ-6. Noorduyn in Canada built a version, similar to the AT-6A except for its R-1340-AN-1 engine: fifteen hun-dred went to the USAAF with the designation AT-16, and two thousand four hundred and eighty-five to the RAF as the Harvard IIB. A small number of Harvard IIB's also served with the Royal Navy. Most of the RAF's Harvard IIA's and III's were utilised in Southern Rhodesia, where, like their counter-parts in Canada, they played a leading role in the giant Empire Air Training Scheme.

34 Miles Martinet

First British service aircraft designed specifically for a target-towing role, the M.25 Martinet was based upon the radial-engined Master II trainer, many components of which were utilised in its design. The first of two Martinet prototypes (LR 241) was flown on 24 April 1942, and one thousand seven hundred and twenty-four production aircraft were subsequently built to Specifi-cation 12/41 for the RAF and Fleet Air Arm. Main external differences from the Master included a lengthened nose, raised cockpit for the two-man crew, and increased wing span. The airframe was strengthened to compensate for the additional equipment and the stresses imposed by drogue towing. The towing gear and targets were stowed in a flat rectangular fairing beneath the centre fuselage, with a wind-driven external winch just beneath the cockpit canopy on the port side. Production continued until 1945, and during the war Martinets were used for communi-cations and air/sea rescue duties in addition to their target-towing activities. In 1943 Martinet PW 979 became the prototype for the M.50 Queen Martinet radio-controlled target drone aircraft. A further seventeen Martinets were similarly converted, and sixty-five more built later from the outset to this configuration. The M.37 Martinet Trainer, with raised rear cockpit, was a development begun during the war, but it was not flown until 1946 and only two conversions were made. After the end of World War 2, small numbers of Martinets were sold to the air forces of Belgium and Eire, and five to a Swedish commercial operator.

35   Junkers Ju 87

The Ju 87 was designed initially as a dive bomber, and first flew in 1935. Early development and production of the Ju 87A, B, C and R bomber variants are described in the *Bombers, Patrol and Transport Aircraft 1939–45* volume in this series. The next major variant to enter production was the Ju 87D, whose evolution had begun in 1940. Several sub-types of this model were built, their chief characteristics being the use of a more powerful Jumo engine, increased fuel tankage similar to that of the Ju 87R, and a considerably refined airframe with reinforced armament and extra armour protection for the crew. Most D variants were evolved for a ground-attack role, and could carry a variety of different weapon loads ranging from a single 3,968 lb (1,800 kg) bomb beneath the fuselage to a pair of underwing pods each containing six 7·9 mm machine-guns. The dive brakes fitted to the earlier Ju 87's were usually omitted. The Ju 87D-5 introduced an extended wing of 49 ft 2½ in (15·00 m) span, and the D-7 was a specialised night-attack version. Variants of the Ju 87D served in the Mediterranean, North Africa and on the Eastern Front, equipping units of the Hungarian and Rumanian air forces as well as those of the *Luftwaffe*. Proposals to replace the D model by developments of it designated Ju 87F and Ju 187 were abandoned in 1943, but one other variant was encountered operationally. This was the Ju 87G, which entered service in 1943 as an anti-tank aeroplane with a 37 mm BK 37 cannon mounted in a streamlined fairing attached beneath each wing. These could be replaced by bombs for more general ground-attack missions. The Ju 87G was essentially a conversion of the long-span D-5, and aircraft of this type were quite successful in knocking out Soviet tanks along the Eastern Front until the appearance of better-class Soviet fighter opposition in the autumn of 1944. Operational trainers for pilots engaged in ground-attack work were produced, under the designation Ju 87H, by converting various D sub-series to have dual controls and modified cockpit hoods. When production of the Ju 87 series finally ended in September 1944, more than five thousand seven hundred of these aircraft had been built.

36   Fairchild PT-19, PT-23 and PT-26

Originating as the Fairchild M-62,

this monoplane primary trainer was a contemporary of the Boeing-Stearman Kaydet biplane, and was ultimately built in almost as great a quantity. First purchases were made in 1940 as part of the US Army Air Corps expansion programme, the initial model having open tandem cockpits and a 175 hp Ranger L-440-1 engine. Two hundred and seventy-five of this model, designated PT-19, were delivered during FY 1940. Mass production then began in 1941 of three thousand one hundred and eighty-one PT-19A's, with 200 hp L-440-3 engines, by Fairchild, with an additional four hundred and seventy-seven by Aeronca and forty-four by the St Louis Aircraft Corporation. Nine hundred and seventeen PT-19B's, built by Fairchild and Aeronca, differed only in being equipped for blind-flying training and having a collapsible canvas hood for the front cockpit. The PT-23, introduced to avoid delays in the supply of sufficient Ranger engines, was essentially the same airframe mounting an uncowled Continental R-670 engine of 220 hp. Eight hundred and sixty-nine PT-23's were completed by Aeronca, Fairchild, Howard Aircraft Corporation and St Louis in the USA and by Fleet Aircraft Corporation in Canada. Howard and St Louis also produced two hundred and fifty-six PT-23A's with blind-flying equipment. For use in Canada in the Empire Air Training Scheme, a variant of the PT-19A was evolved with a fully-enclosed canopy for the two occupants. Fairchild contributed six hundred and

seventy, with L-440-3 engines, to the RCAF under Lend-Lease, and production of eight hundred and seven PT-26A's and two hundred and fifty PT-26B's by Fleet, with L-440-7 engines, was also financed by US funds. The Canadian-built PT-26 and PT-26A aircraft were designated Cornell I and II, and were used at RAF flying schools in Southern Rhodesia as well as in Canada.

37 Miles Magister

The Tiger Moth and the Magister elementary trainers may be regarded as the British counterparts of the Kaydet and the Fairchild PT-19 series, although the Magister was built in by no means the quantity of the American monoplane. Nevertheless, what it lacked in numbers the 'Maggie' more than made up for in appeal, and many hundreds of British and Commonwealth pilots remember their training on Magisters with something akin to affection. The Magister was first introduced into RAF service in October 1937, a descendant of the civil Hawk Major (an example of which had undergone service evaluation in 1936) and other members of the Hawk family. It was the first monoplane *ab initio* trainer to be accepted for RAF service, and later served extensively with the Fleet Air Arm as well. To Specification 37/37, production was initiated early in 1937, and continued until 1941, when one thousand two hundred and three Magisters had been built. About three-fifths of this total were already in service by 3 September 1939.

After the outbreak of World War 2 these were augmented by many more Magisters, and other Miles two-seaters, impressed from the British Civil Register, and the type was employed at most RAF Elementary Flying Training Schools. The Magister was a fully aerobatic aeroplane, and could be equipped for blind-flying training, when a canvas hood was provided for the rear cockpit. Most of those in war-time service dispensed with the mainwheel 'spat' fairings to facilitate maintenance. Substantial numbers returned to civilian flying in the UK after the war, when the type was renamed Hawk Trainer III, and many others were exported.

38 Ilyushin Il-2

Probably the most advanced and most effective ground-attack air-craft to see service during World War 2, the Il-2 *Shturmovik*, like the Junkers Ju 87 before it, introduced a new word into the terminology of combat aircraft. After extensive study of several proposals by a number of design teams, those of the Ilyushin bureau were accepted, and materialised in the BSh-2 (or TsKB-55) prototype, which flew for the first time on 30 December 1939. About fifteen per cent of its total weight consisted of armour-plate protection for the engine, fuel and cooling systems and the two-man crew, and tests with the first two prototypes indicated insufficient engine power and a lack of longi-tudinal stability. The original 1,370 hp AM-35 engine was therefore replaced, in a modified prototype

(TsKB-57), by the new 1,680 hp AM-38 which offered much greater power for take-off and low altitude flying. The TsKB-57 was a single-seater, with improved armament and capable of carrying several alternative external warloads; it flew for the first time on 12 October 1940. This version entered pro-duction, as the Il-2, in the following spring, and carried out its first operational engagements in the summer of 1941. Output of aircraft and engines increased rapidly, the number of Il-2's in service being quadrupled by mid-1943. By this time a modified version was in pro-duction, in which a second crew member was restored to man a rear-firing gun, and which had improved take-off performance, manoeuvra-bility and anti-tank weapons. This model, designated Il-2m3, entered production in mid-1942 and became operational in the following October. By early 1943 the 2-seat version was scoring heavily in air-to-air combat even against the German Bf 109's, and with masterly understatement the official trials report declared that it could 'be introduced with ad-vantage into ground-attack units'. The improved anti-tank weapons and 37 mm cannon carried by later-production Il-2m3's main-tained the aircraft's effectiveness even against the new German Panther and Tiger tanks in the summer of 1943, and flying per-formance was sustained by intro-duction of the 1,750 hp AM-48F engine in later production batches. The total quantity built – estimated at about thirty-five thousand – would alone make the Il-2 an outstanding aeroplane, but its intrinsic merits had no need of academic support, and its achievements were their own recommendation.

39 Boulton Paul Defiant

The Defiant was designed to Air Ministry Specification F.9/35, which called for a 2-seat fighter in which the entire armament was concentrated in a power-operated, centrally mounted turret permitting a 360° radius of fire in the hemisphere above the aeroplane. The theory was that such a fighter would be useful for attacking enemy bomber formations from below: how it was to defend itself in the event of similar attack is apparently not recorded! The first of two prototypes (K 8310) was flown – minus the turret – on 11 August 1937, and the Boulton Paul design was selected in preference to its only remaining competitor, the Hawker Hotspur; indeed, the initial order for eighty-seven was placed before either type had flown. Despite excellent flying characteristics, the Defiant's early trials programme was protracted, and only three had been delivered by the outbreak of war, although orders by then had increased to well over four hundred. The first RAF squadron to equip with Defiant I day fighters (1,036 hp Merlin III engine) was No 264 in December 1939, which carried out its first operational sorties on 12 May 1940. The next day, five out of a flight of six were destroyed by Bf 109E's that had attacked them in their weakest quarters – from ahead and below.

Then, by flying mixed formations of Defiants and Hurricanes – to which the Defiant bore a considerable resemblance – enemy pilots were for a while deceived into diving from behind on to what they believed to be defenceless Hurricanes, only to be met by a stream of fire from the Defiant's four Browning guns. However, the effectiveness of this chase-me-so-I-can-hit-you policy was short-lived, and soon the Defiant was transferred to night-fighting operations, equipped with the newly developed airborne interception radar. The Defiant II, with AI Mk IV radar, and Merlin XX engine, entered squadron service in September 1941, though in comparatively small numbers, but the night-fighter Defiants were appreciably more successful than the type had been on daytime operations, accounting for more enemy aircraft during the winter *blitz* of 1940–41 than any other type. Two hundred and seven Defiant II's were built, compared with seven hundred and thirteen Mk I's. In 1942, however, the Defiant's role as a fighter ended. A number were transferred to air/sea rescue, training and other secondline duties, but the main task ahead of the aircraft was now that of a target tug. One hundred and forty Defiant III's were manufactured (without turrets) for this role, in addition to which many more exfighter Mks I and II were converted to similar configuration. Defiant DR 994 had the distinction of being fitted with the first-ever Martin-Baker ejection seat, with which the first dummy ejection trials were carried out in May 1945, and one other machine was later used for similar trials.

40 Dewoitine 520

Design of the D.520, by Robert Castello, was initiated by Dewoitine in mid-1936 as a private venture. After some initial lack of enthusiasm, the French ordered two prototypes of a modified version in April 1938 from the SNCA du Midi, which by then had absorbed the Dewoitine company. The first of these was flown on 2 October 1938, powered by an 860 hp Hispano-Suiza 12Y-21 engine, and in later trials with a 12Y-29 engine it attained its design speed of 373 mph (520 km/hr). The second prototype carried armament and incorporated a number of structural and aerodynamic improvements, including redesigned tail surfaces. An initial order was placed in April 1939 for two hundred D.520's, and successive orders (and cancellations) up to April 1940 required a total of two thousand two hundred to be built for the *Armée de l'Air* and one hundred and twenty for the *Aéronavale*. Production aircraft, with a slightly longer fuselage, increased fuel tankage and armour protection for the pilot, were powered by Hispano-Suiza 12Y-45 engines, and began to be delivered to an experimental flight at Bricy in January 1940. When the German offensive in France began on 10 May 1940, only thirty-six D.520's were in service, with *Groupe de Chasse* I/3. These fought their first actions against the *Luftwaffe* on 13 May. In all, D.520's served with five *Groupes de Chasse* during the May–June fighting, destroying well over a hundred enemy aircraft for a loss of fifty-four of their own number due to enemy action. After 25 June 1940, well over three hundred D.520's (of four hundred and thirty-seven then built) survived either in unoccupied France or in North Africa, and the latter were utilised by four *Groupes* of the Vichy French Air Force and one *Escadrille* of the *Aéronavale*. In 1941 the German authorities ordered the production of five hundred and fifty more D.520's, although only three hundred and forty-nine of these were actually completed. In 1943–44, following the occupation of the remainder of France and the disbandment of the Vichy Air Force, the SNCA du Sud-Est completed a further quantity for German use, bringing overall production of the D.520 to nine hundred and five aircraft. In addition to the *Luftwaffe*, the air forces of Bulgaria, Italy and Rumania were also supplied with quantities of the French fighters. Aircraft recaptured by the Allies, as France was progressively liberated, fought with the *Forces Françaises de l'Interieur* during the final months of the war in Europe.

41 Miles Master

The Master was evolved from the Miles Kestrel trainer which, when it made its public debut at Hendon in July 1937, attracted considerable attention on account of its clean, fighter-like lines and the maximum speed of 295 mph (475 km/hr) which it could reach with its 745 hp

Rolls-Royce Kestrel XVI engine. The production Master I, ordered in June 1938, incorporated detail modifications to the airframe, but was a heavier aeroplane and powered by the lower-rated 715 hp Kestrel XXX. Nevertheless it remained one of the fastest trainers of its time anywhere in the world, was sturdily built and fully aerobatic. The first production Master I (N 7408) was flown on 31 March 1939, and deliveries to the RAF began just before the outbreak of war. Nine hundred Mks I and IA were built, the latter version having a slightly modified windscreen. This total also included twenty-five aircraft completed as M.24 emergency fighters during the Battle of Britain, and several Master I's for the Fleet Air Arm. Cessation of Kestrel engine production, coupled with the ever-increasing numbers of radial-engined aircraft entering British service, led to large orders for the Master II, whose prototype (N 7422) had flown on 30 October 1939. This was essentially a Mk I airframe adapted to take an 870 hp Bristol Mercury XX air-cooled radial, and production of the Master I eventually totalled one thousand seven hundred and ninety-nine. This version was used for general training duties, many later being converted as glider tugs. The prevalence of US Lend-Lease aircraft in British service led to the third basic model, first flown on 27 November 1940. This was the Master III, which differed from the Mk I primarily in having an 825 hp Pratt & Whitney R-1535-SB4-G Twin Wasp Junior engine. The American engine, although a two-row radial and heavier than the single-row Mercury, was of smaller diameter; hence the extra weight was offset by a reduction in drag, and performance remained virtually unaffected. Six hundred and two Master III's were completed before production ceased in favour of the Martinet in 1942. During the early months of 1942 the original duo-curved wingtips of all Master variants were clipped by 20·5 in (0·52 m) on each side and squared off, to relieve stress on the centre-section occasioned by the gull-wing configuration. Manoeuvrability was slightly increased as a result, at little cost to the aircraft's ceiling and rate of climb.

42 Yakovlev Yak-9

The Yak-9, which itself was produced in a number of variants, represented the culmination of a highly successful line of single-engined fighters and trainers from the Yakovlev design bureau whose combined production total was in the region of thirty thousand aircraft. It stemmed from the I-26 prototype of 1938 (which became the Yak-1 in production two years later), via the Yak-7, and the machines which acted as Yak-9 prototypes were originally designated Yak-7DI, signifying that they were designed as long-range fighters. They appeared in the first half of 1942, differing from the standard Yak-7B fighter chiefly in making greater use of light alloys in their construction. Production began in the autumn of 1942, and the Yak-9 was in operational service by the turn of the year in the fighting around Stalingrad. In 1943 the Yak-9 began to be used as an anti-tank aircraft, being modified for this purpose as the Yak-9T to carry a 37 mm cannon or a lighter weapon in the forward part of the fuselage. This was followed in 1944 by the Yak-9K, mounting a 45 mm cannon that fired through the propeller shaft. The Yak-9B was a fighter-bomber version equipped to carry a 992 lb (450 kg) bomb internally, and in 1943–44 the Yak-9D and Yak-9DD emerged as variants with their range further increased to proved fighter cover for advancing troops and for bombing raids over enemy-held territory. One squadron of these, flying from southern Italy after the Italian armistice, provided support for the partisan forces in Yugoslavia, and other Yak-9 variants served with Polish and French units (including the celebrated Normandie-Niemen group) fighting in the USSR. The last major version to serve during the war period was the all-metal Yak-9U, which flew in prototype form in January 1944. This became operational during the second half of that year and was characterised chiefly by further aerodynamic refinements and the adoption of the new 1,600 hp VK-107A engine which raised the fighter's top speed to 435 mph (700 km/hr). The Yak-9U could climb from sea level to 16,400 ft (5,000 m) in nearly half a minute less than the Messerschmitt Bf 109G. The final Yak-9 variant (originally known briefly as the Yak-11) was the Yak-9P, which appeared in 1945. This saw comparatively little service in World War 2, but was a standard post-war fighter and fighter-bomber with Soviet and satellite air forces, including the North Korean Air Force during 1950–53.

43 Mikoyan & Gurevich MiG-3

The first fighter aeroplane to be produced by the now-famous Mikoyan-Gurevich design bureau originated under the designation I-200. Work on this project, which was for a high-altitude fighter, began late in 1939, and the prototype was flown on 5 April 1940, powered by a 1,200 hp (at altitude) Mikulin AM-35A engine. The aircraft was of mixed metal and wood construction, and lightly armed with one 12·7 mm and two 7·62 mm machine-guns. It entered production, as the MiG-1, late in 1940, but in the following year the design was modified to become the MiG-3. The redesigned fighter featured a sliding canopy for the previously open cockpit, improved rearward vision for the pilot, extra internal tankage, increased outer-wing dihedral and the radiator bath extended further forward under the fuselage. Production was extremely modest by Soviet wartime standards – only some two thousand one hundred MiG-1's and MiG-3's were built – and, despite an excellent high-altitude performance, the MiG-3's effectiveness as a combat machine was limited. At lower altitudes, although manoeuvrable, it could not fly or climb a ast as its *Luftwaffe* opponents, and it was lacking in firepower. The latter weakness was recognised later by equipping the fighter with an additional 12·7 mm gun beneath each wing, but the extra weight of these and the increased armour protection added simultaneously served only to detract still further from the MiG-3's performance. Production of the MiG-3 ceased, with that of the AM-35A engine, at the end of 1941.

4 North American P-51 Mustang

The Mustang was first conceived to meet a British requirement for a high-speed fighter posed in April 1940, and was evolved by a design team led by Raymond Rice and Edgar Schmued. With the manufacturer's designation NA-73, the prototype (registered NX 19998) made its first flight on 26 October 1940 powered by a 1,100 hp Allison V-1710-F3R engine. The initial British orders were for six hundred and twenty Mustang I's, the first of which reached the UK in November 1941. Two similar aircraft were evaluated by the US Army as XP-51's, after which one hundred and fifty P-51's were ordered for Lend-Lease to the RAF as Mustang IA's. In the event, fifty-five of these were repossessed by the USAAF and converted to F-6A photo-reconnaissance aircraft, while two others became XP-78's (later XP-51B's) when fitted in 1942 with Packard-built Merlin engines. (This followed similar British experiments with Merlin 60 series engines fitted in four Mustang I's.) The Merlin was

to become the Mustang's standard powerplant on both sides of the Atlantic, but before this the USAAF received five hundred examples of an Allison-engined ground-attack variant, the A-36A, and three hundred and ten P-51A's, also Allison-powered. The RAF received fifty P-51A's (Mustang II), and thirty-five others were converted to F-6B's. The A-36A was briefly named Invader (and the P-51 named Apache), but the British name Mustang was later adopted for all P-51 variants. One A-36A was evaluated by the RAF, but no production aircraft were received. First Merlin-engined production models were the P-51B and P-51C (RAF Mustang III), the combined US production of which totalled three thousand seven hundred and thirty-eight. The nine hundred and ten supplied to the RAF were fitted with bulged cockpit hoods to improve visibility. Ninety-one US conversions of P-51B/C Mustangs into F-6C's were carried out. A major design change appeared with the P-51D, in which the rear fuselage was cut down to permit the fitting of a 'teardrop' cockpit canopy affording all-round vision. Production totalled nine thousand two hundred and ninety-three of this model and the basically similar P-51K. Eight hundred and seventy-six became Mustang IV's with the RAF, and two hundred and ninety-nine became reconnaissance F-6D's or F-6K's. Next production model was the P-51H, five hundred and fifty-five of which were completed in 1945 before outstanding contracts for more than another three thousand Mustangs were cancelled at the war's end. The first RAF Mustangs became operational, in an armed tactical reconnaissance capacity, in July 1942, while from December 1943 P-51B's of the USAAF flew in increasing numbers as escorts to Eighth Air Force bombers during raids over Europe. The Mustang also figured largely in the Allied campaigns in North Africa, against V1 flying bombs over Britain in 1944 and as escort during the B-29 bombing raids of 1944–45 against Japan. Unquestionably, it was one of the greatest and most versatile fighters ever built, and a firm favourite with all who flew it; as the British journal *The Aeroplane* commented in July 1942: 'Pilots who fly the Mustang praise it so lavishly that they exhaust their superlatives before they have finished their eulogies.'

45 Kawasaki Ki-61 Hien (Swallow)

Two designs were formulated by Dr Takeo Doi to meet a February 1940 fighter requirement of the JAAF: the Ki-60 'heavy' fighter and the lightweight Ki-61. Three prototypes of the former were completed, but the Ki-60 was then discarded for the more conventional Ki-61 design. Twelve Ki-61 prototypes were built, all similar in their essential features, and the first of them was flown in December 1941. It was powered by a 1,100 hp Ha-140 liquid-cooled engine, evolved in Japan from the German DB 601A, and this later gave rise to the erroneous assump-

tion that the Ki-61 was a licence-built development of the Messerschmitt Bf 109. The initial production model, delivery of which began in August 1942, was the Ki-61-I Model 1, which was armed with two 12·7 mm and two 7·7 mm guns. Successive improvements in armament led to the Model 1A (two 7·7 mm fuselage guns and two 20 mm wing-mounted Mauser cannon), Model 1B (four 12·7 mm guns), Model 1C (two fuselage 12·7 mm and two 20 mm Ho-5 in the wings) and Model 1D (two fuselage 12·7 mm and two 30 mm in the wings). Total production of the Ki-61-I series fighters amounted to two thousand seven hundred and thirty-four. Following its first operational appearance in New Guinea in April 1943, the Hien (Allied code name 'Tony') was encountered in virtually all battle areas of the Pacific war. It was particularly prominent around Rabaul, in the battle for Leyte Island, and in the home defence of Japan. In September 1942, to offset certain maintenance difficulties encountered with the Ha-40 engine, Kawasaki began to evolve the Ki-61-II, utilising the new Ha-140 which promised to develop 1,450 hp. The first Ki-61-II Model 2, completed in August 1943, featured a lengthened fuselage, modified canopy and a ten per cent increase in wing area. However, difficulties with the Ha-140 engine and associated structural problems prevented more than another seven from being completed by January 1944. Attention was then devoted to the Ki-61-IIa Model 2A, with strengthened

rframe and the wings and armament of the Ki-61-Ic. The Model 2B
was similar except in having four
20 mm guns. However, after only
thirty-one Model 2A's and 2B's had
been completed, output was slowed
down because it was fast outpacing
that of the necessary powerplants.
Another three hundred and seventy-
four Ki-61 airframes were completed, but only ninety-nine of them
received their intended powerplants
and more than one-third of those
were destroyed in air attacks before
delivery. The remainder were eventually fitted with 1,500 hp Mitsubishi Ha-112-II radial engines to
become Ki-100's, and in this form
were so successful that further
development of the proposed Ki-61-
II was rendered unnecessary.

46 & 47 Hawker Hurricane

The first monoplane in an historic
cavalcade of Hawker fighters, the
Hurricane, perhaps more than any
other type, is indissolubly associated
with the name of its designer, Sydney Camm. Its evolution began in
1933 as a monoplane development
of the Fury biplane fighter, to have
a fixed landing gear and a Rolls-
Royce Goshawk engine. Early in
1934, however, significant improvement of the design included a fully
retractable main undercarriage, provision for eight wing-mounted machine-guns and the decision to use
the new Rolls-Royce PV-12 engine
that later became the Merlin. To
specification F.36/34, Hawker completed an unarmed prototype (K
5083), powered by a Merlin C
engine, which flew for the first time

on 6 November 1935. In March 1936,
anticipating the first RAF orders
by some three months, Hawker
began to prepare for an initial
production of one thousand of the
fighters – a piece of foresight whose
value was emphasised when the
Battle of Britain was fought some
four years later. The initial RAF
order was for six hundred Hurricane
I's, and delivery of these began, to
No 111 Squadron, in October 1937.
On 3 September 1939 there were
three hundred and fifteen Hurricanes on the fully operational
strength of fourteen RAF squadrons,
plus others in reserve, and total
orders stood at three thousand five
hundred. Eventual production of
the Hurricane I, shared between
Hawker and Gloster factories in the
UK and the Canadian Car and
Foundry Co of Montreal, amounted
to three thousand nine hundred and
fifty-four. Powerplant was originally
the Merlin II, later the Merlin III;
the Canadian-built machines were
later redesignated Mk X. Unlike
the Spitfire, the Hurricane became
operational with the Advanced Air
Striking Force in France at the outset of World War 2, and it outnumbered the Spitfire by about two
to one in the Battle of Britain in
August–October 1940. During the
second half of 1940 the Hurricane I
began to appear in the Middle East,
following the entry of Italy into the
war; these aircraft (and later
Hurricanes serving in North Africa)
were characterised by the distinctive
Vokes sand filter beneath the nose.
In 1942, Hurricanes also made their
operational appearance in the Far

East, in Singapore, the Netherlands East Indies and Burma, and were operating also in the fighter-bomber role. Meanwhile, on 11 June 1940, Hurricane P 3269 had flown with a 1,185 hp supercharged Merlin XX engine to serve as prototype for the Mk II. Early production aircraft, retaining the standard 8-gun wings, were designated Mk IIA; with twelve machine-guns the designation became Mk IIB, while the Mk IIC had a wing armament of four 20 mm cannon. Acknowledgment that the Hurricane was becoming outclassed as a fighter came in 1942 with the increasing use of the aircraft for ground-attack duties. Several Hurricane IIC's were equipped to carry underwing rocket projectiles, and the Mk IID was a special anti-tank version with two 40 mm underwing cannon and two Brownings in the wings. The only other British production model, the Mk IV, was also a ground-attack type, with a variety of possible weapon arrangements and a 1,620 hp Merlin 24 or 27 engine. The other major operational form of the aircraft was the Sea Hurricane, equipped with catapult spools and (except for the first fifty Mk IA's) an arrester hook. This first appeared in 1941 as an interim step to protect convoys from the attentions of U-boats and prowling Fw 200 maritime patrol bombers, and the Sea Hurricanes were carried on board CAM ships (Catapult Aircraft Merchantmen). Once launched, they had to 'ditch' in the sea after an engagement in the hope of the pilot being picked up by another ship in the convoy.

Conversion of existing Hurrican resulted in Sea Hurricanes Mks IA IB, IC and XIIA. The Mk IIC ha a 1,460 hp Merlin XX and full Flee Air Arm radio and other equipmen but no catapult spools. The tota number of Sea Hurricanes built o converted was about eight hundred Overall Hurricane production in th UK was thirteen thousand an eighty by Hawker, Gloster an Austin Motors; the Canadian Ca and Foundry Co built additiona Mk X, as well as Mks XI, XII an XIIA, with various armaments an Packard-Merlin engines, to a tota of one thousand four hundred an fifty-one, making a grand total o fourteen thousand five hundred an thirty-three Hurricanes of all kind Two thousand nine hundred an fifty-two Hurricanes were allocate to the Soviet Air Force during th early years of the war, althoug many of these were lost en route.

48 Messerschmitt Bf 109
The Bf 109 was designed in respons to a 1933 RLM specification by th Bayerische Flugzeugwerke, the ori ginal concept being based on the us of the 610 hp Junkers Jumo 210A engine, which was then the mos powerful developed in Germany. A example of this engine was no available in time for the first fligh of the prototype (D-IABI), whic flew instead in September 1935 wit a Rolls-Royce Kestrel V. In Januar 1936 the second machine was flow with the Jumo engine, and by the ten aircraft had been ordered by th RLM for evaluation. The propose two-gun Bf 109A did not go int

roduction, the first series model being the Bf 109B-1 (635 hp Jumo 10D) armed either with three MG 7 guns or two MG 17's and an MG F, the latter firing through the propeller shaft. A team of Bf 109's scored several successes at Zürich in 1937, and on 11 November that year the Bf 109V13, with a specially boosted DB 601 engine, established a new world landplane speed record of 379·38 mph (610·55 km/hr). Twenty-four Bf 109B-2's were despatched in 1937 to join the *Luftwaffe*'s Condor Legion in Spain, followed soon after by others of the same model. The Bf 109C-1, which joined them in 1938, had the number of guns increased to five. Some E-2 aircraft were converted to Bf 109D-0's by the installation of DB 601A engines, and small numbers of the similarly powered D-1 were exported to Hungary and Switzerland. By this time five other German manufacturers had joined the production programme, and two hundred and thirty-five Bf 109D series fighters were in *Luftwaffe* service at the outbreak of World War 2. They were already being replaced in increasing numbers, however, by the Bf 109E series which first appeared in 1938. This series proved to be superior in performance and manoeuvrability to virtually every type of fighter opposed to it during the advances through Poland, Czechoslovakia, France, Belgium and Holland, and Bf 109E production mounted so rapidly that Germany could afford to export substantial numbers of the Bf 109E-3 in 1939–40 to Bulgaria (nineteen), Hungary (forty), Japan (two), Rumania (sixty-nine), Slovakia (sixteen), Switzerland (eighty), the USSR (five) and Yugoslavia (seventy-three). Despite these claims on the numbers built, the Bf 109E remained the principal *Luftwaffe* version in service throughout the Battle of Britain. The E series extended to the E-9, and included models built as fighters, fighter-bombers and reconnaissance aircraft. In July 1940 Fieseler began converting ten E-3's to Bf 109T (*Träger* = carrier) configuration for operation from the proposed aircraft carrier *Graf Zeppelin*, but this project proved abortive and they were restored to their original configuration late in 1941. The finest model of the Bf 109 was the Bf 109F, the first version capable of out-manoeuvring the Spitfire V and a much cleaner design aerodynamically. The F series were powered by either 1,200 hp DB 601N or 1,300 hp DB 601E engines, with neater nose contours, the tail assembly redesign included a cantilever tailplane and retractable tailwheel, and the increased-span wings had rounded-off tips. By the late summer of 1942, however, the F series had been supplanted in production and service by the Bf 109G, familiarly known as the 'Gustav'. This was the last major production model, and was intended to be an improved version of the Bf 109F. In fact, the heavier DB 605 engine and extra equipment installed brought an inevitable drop in performance; but despite this, the production rate actually increased, and the Bf 109G was widely employed in Europe, North Africa and on the Russo-German front. More than fourteen thousand Bf 109's – nearly half of the total German production of the type – were built in 1944 alone, and G models were exported to Bulgaria (one hundred and forty-five), Finland (one hundred and sixty-two), Hungary (fifty-nine), Japan (two), Rumania (seventy), Slovakia (fifteen), Spain (twenty-five) and Switzerland (twelve). The Bf 109H was an extended-span high-altitude version built only in small numbers, and the Bf 109K (a refined version of the G) likewise saw only limited service. Projected versions included the Bf 109L and Bf 109S, neither of which reached production status. Licence production of the German fighter continued after the war in Czechoslovakia and Spain, and when this too came to an end an approximate total of thirty-five thousand Bf 109-type fighters had been built; between 1936 and 1945, production of this aircraft represented nearly two-thirds of Germany's entire output of single-seat fighters.

49 Macchi C.202 Folgore (Thunderbolt)

Attempts to improve the performance of the C.200 Saetta fighter (q.v.) began as early as 1938, when Macchi evolved the C.201 by redesigning the fuselage with the object of installing a 1,000 hp Fiat A.76 RC 40 radial engine. When development of this engine was abandoned the C.201 was testflown with a standard Saetta engine,

but the project was then discarded in favour of the more promising C.202. This resulted from the acquisition in 1940 of a specimen of the German Daimler-Benz DB 601A-1 liquid-cooled inverted-Vee engine, which was installed in a C.200 airframe (MM 445) to create the prototype of the C.202. This machine flew for the first time on 10 August 1940, and the advance over the C.200, both aerodynamically and in terms of performance, was such that immediate production of the new fighter was authorised. Initially, production C.202's were powered by DB 601 engines imported from Germany, but soon these engines began to be licence built in Italy for the Folgore as the Alfa Romeo RA.1000 RC 41. Production of the C.200 and C.202 continued in parallel, and the first examples of the Folgore began to enter service with the *Regia Aeronautica* in the summer of 1941. At first, they carried similar armament to the Saetta, but later batches had two additional 7·7 mm wing guns and one was tested with a 20 mm Mauser MG 151 cannon in a fairing beneath each wing. The Folgore is generally considered the most effective Italian fighter of the war period, and served in the Mediterranean, North Africa and on the Eastern Front. It remained in production until the Italian armistice in September 1943, though the quantity manufactured was somewhat restricted by the output rate of the engines to power it. Macchi built three hundred and ninety-two and about eleven hundred more

vere completed by Breda. The
C.205V Veltro (Greyhound) was a
much-improved development with a
,475 hp DB 605A engine, but
became available too late to take
any major part in the war.

0   Bell P-63 Kingcobra

The Kingcobra, developed from the
P-39 Airacobra, originated in April
1941 when three XP-39E prototypes
vere ordered, utilising the P-39D
fuselage allied to new, angular tail
surfaces, an Allison V-1710-47 engine and a completely redesigned
laminar-flow wing. Two months
later two additional prototypes,
designated XP-63 (Bell Model 33)
vere ordered; these incorporated
further modifications, and the first
of them (41-9511) made its maiden
flight on 7 December 1942. A third
prototype (XP-63A) was flown in
April 1943, and in the following
October delivery began of the first
of one thousand seven hundred and
twenty-five production P-63A's, in
several sub-series which differed
chiefly in their armament or other
equipment. Provision was made for
various external stores, including
bombs, rocket projectiles or auxiliary fuel tanks. The XP-63B was a
proposed version (subsequently cancelled) with a Packard-built Merlin
engine, but the next to go into
production was the P-63C, which
had additional fin area beneath the
rear fuselage and a V-1710-117
engine; one thousand two hundred
and twenty-seven P-63C's were
completed. One P-63D, thirteen
P-63E's (increased wing span) and
one P-39F were completed in 1945,

and the final total of all P-63
variants built by 1946 was three
thousand three hundred and three.
None are known to have served
operationally with the USAAF, but
two thousand four hundred and
twenty-one P-63A's and P-63C's
were allocated under Lend-Lease
arrangements to the Soviet Air
Force, with whom they rendered
excellent service, chiefly as ground-
attack aircraft. Three hundred
P-63C's were supplied to the Free
French Air Force (FAFL), and
more than three hundred others
were used in the USA as armoured
target aircraft.

51   Bell P-39 Airacobra

Originating as the Bell Model 12,
the Airacobra was designed by
Robert J. Woods primarily as a
vehicle for a heavy-calibre cannon.
Installation of this gun in the
optimum firing position – in the
nose, along the aircraft's centre line
– dictated the fighter's radical
configuration whereby the engine
was installed amidships, aft of the
cockpit, to drive the propeller by
means of a long extension shaft.
When one XP-39 prototype was
ordered in October 1937 the Bell
fighter achieved the further distinction of becoming the first single-
engined fighter ordered by the
USAAC to be fitted with a tricycle
landing gear. The XP-39 flew for
the first time on 6 April 1939, a
contract for thirteen YP-39 test
aircraft being awarded later that
month. These were based on the
prototype, after its modification to
XP-39B standard without the engine

supercharger originally fitted. The first production version was the P-39C, but only twenty of these were completed. In the P-39D, the 37 mm cannon and twin 0·50 in guns in the nose were supplemented by four 0·30 in wing-mounted machine-guns and provision was made for an external bomb or fuel tank to be carried. Four hundred and four P-39D's were built for the US Army, delivery beginning in April 1941. A further four hundred and ninety-four P-39D-1 and D-2 Airacobras (Bell Model 14) were built for Lend-Lease allocations, these having a nose cannon of lighter (20 mm) calibre. Plans by Britain to buy six hundred and seventy-five Airacobras were by no means fully realised: many were lost during delivery and more than two hundred were instead made available to the Soviet Air Force, while the USAAF, after Pearl Harbor, repossessed a similar quantity which it designated P-400. Only one RAF squadron (No 600) became operational with the Airacobra, but those of the USAAF were soon in action against the Japanese in theatres as far afield as Alaska, Hawaii, Panama and the south-west Pacific. During the latter half of 1942 they also became operational over Europe and in North Africa, and were particularly effective in the latter theatre in the ground-attack role. Numerous further variants appeared, the differences between which principally concerned the variant of V-1710 engine and type of propeller fitted; they included the P-39F, J, K, L, M, N and Q. The last of these introduced a change of armament, replacing the four 0·3 in wing guns by two of 0·50 in calibre. The two most widely built models were the P-39N (two thous and and ninety-five) and the P-39Q (four thousand nine hundred and five). Entire production of the Airacobra, ending in 1944, was undertaken by Bell, who built a total, including experimental machines, of nine thousand five hundred and fifty-eight. Well over half this total, mostly P-39N's and P-39Q's, were allocated to the Soviet Union: nearly two hundred of these were lost en route, but four thousand seven hundred and fifty-eight arrived safely to render excellent service on the Eastern Front between 1942 and 1945.

52 Hawker Typhoon

The Typhoon was evolved by Sydney Camm's design staff at Hawker Aircraft in response to Air Ministry Specification F.18/37 which was for an interceptor capable of combating such heavily armed and armoured escort fighters as the Messerschmitt Bf 110. Such an aeroplane was inevitably heavier than either the Hurricane or the Spitfire, and to provide a comparable performance the powerplants selected were the new Napier Sabre H-type in-line engine and the X-type Rolls-Royce Vulture, both of which promised to develop some 2,000 hp. Prototypes were completed with both types of engine: the Vulture-engined design, named Tornado, was later abandoned when Vulture production was curtailed

With the Sabre engine, the aircraft was named Typhoon, and the first of two prototypes (P 5212) was flown on 24 February 1940. Early service trials and squadron experience were far short of being satisfactory, and it is conceivable that the Typhoon's future career might soon have ended but for the appearance in 1941 of the Focke-Wulf Fw 190 in hit-and-run raids across the English Channel. The Fw 190 could out-manoeuvre all other British fighters, including the Spitfire V, and the Typhoon was the only effective means of stopping it. The early Typhoon IA's carried six 0·303 in Browning guns in each wing, but these were replaced in the Mk IB by four wing-mounted 20 mm cannon, which became the Typhoon's regular fixed armament. The fighter was unspectacular at altitude, but its clashes with the Fw 190 had revealed outstanding strength and agility at low level, and from this stemmed the type's widespread use – and success – as a ground-attack aircraft. After extensive weapons trials during 1942, Typhoons began to be fitted for operational use in the following year with underwing rails for eight rocket projectiles, the chief weapon employed by the type. Before and after the invasion of Europe, rocket-armed Typhoons attacked land and sea targets in the Channel and in Belgium, France and the Netherlands. A total of three thousand three hundred and thirty Typhoons were built, all by Gloster except for the two proto-types, five Mk IA's and ten Mk IB's. The Typhoon IB represented the major version, over three thousand being completed with Sabre IIA, IIB or IIC engines, some sixty per cent of this total having bubble-type canopies in place of the original frame-type cockpit hood and car-type access door.

53 Hawker Tempest

The Tempest, originating as the P.1012, was originally given the name Typhoon II, but despite a certain external similarity to the Typhoon IB the P.1012 was virtually a new design, evolved specifically to overcome the performance difficulties of its predecessor. Two prototypes were built to Specification F.10/41, and the first of these (HM 595) was flown on 2 September 1942 with a Napier Sabre V engine. A Sabre IV powered the second machine, but contracts for four hundred similarly powered Tempest I's were later amended to a Sabre II-engined version, which as the Tempest V was the first to enter production. This proved to be the only Tempest to see operational wartime service, designated Mk V Series I with a Sabre IIA and Mk V Series IIB with a Sabre IIB and fully buried guns. The first Tempests were delivered to No 3 Squadron RAF and No 486 Squadron RNZAF in April 1944, and flew many cross-Channel sorties before and after the invasion of Normandy. Soon after the invasion, they rapidly became one of the principal fighters employed to combat the VI flying bombs over southern England, accounting for more than one-third of those destroyed. Eight hundred

Tempest V's were built. The Mk VI (one hundred and forty-two built) was an improved model with Sabre V engine, but did not see service until after the war. Neither did the Tempest II, chronologically the last serving version, which was powered by a 2,520 hp Bristol Centaurus V or VI radial engine. Four hundred and seventy-two Tempest II's were completed, this model remaining in RAF service until 1951 and with the Indian and Pakistan air forces until 1953. The Tempest V and VI were relegated to target-towing duties in the early post-war period.

54 Fairey Fulmar

This 2-seat carrier-borne fighter, the first eight-gun combat aeroplane to serve with the British Fleet Air Arm, was adapted from a lightweight variant of the Battle day bomber produced by Fairey in 1936. Specification O.8/38 was issued to cover a fighter version of this design, but no separate prototype was built. The first flight was made on 4 January 1940 by N 1854, which was the first aircraft of the initial production order. The first squadron to receive the Fulmar I was No 806, in July 1940 – after an uncommonly rapid service trials programme – and a month or two later this squadron had become operational aboard HMS *Illustrious* in the Mediterranean. In all, the Fulmar served with fourteen FAA squadrons, despite the modest numbers built. These comprised two hundred and fifty Mk I's with 1,080 hp Merlin VIII engines, and three hundred and fifty Mk II's powered by the 1,300 hp

Merlin 30 and incorporating equip ment for operation in tropic climates. Despite a useful armamen and range, the Fulmar's perform ance was well below that of contem porary land-based fighters. It wa used with some success on nigh convoy escort and night intrude duties during the middle war year but was superseded in the carrie based day fighter role by Seafir and other single-seat types fro 1942 onward.

55 Fairey Firefly

Conceived early in 1940 as a extremely advanced 2-seat Flee fighter, the Fairey Firefly sav comparatively little of its tota squadron service during World Wa 2, but it was to remain a standar FAA type, in much-altered form until the late 1950s. The Faire design, evolved under H. E. Chap lin, received official Admiralt approval in June 1940, when tw hundred Fireflies were ordered t Specification N.5/40. The prototyp (Z 1826) was flown on 22 Decembe 1941, was armed with four 20 mn cannon and, despite being nearl two tons heavier than the earlie Fulmar, was some 40 mph (6 km/hr) faster, thanks to its superio aerodynamic qualities and a 1,73 hp Griffon IIB engine. Three furthe prototypes were completed, an deliveries of production Firefly Mk I's began in March 1943 although it was July 1944 befor the type became operational, wit No 1770 Squadron (HMS *Indefatig able*), in the attacks upon th German battleship *Tirpitz*. Fou hundred and twenty-nine F Mk I's, built by Fairey and General Aircraft Ltd, were followed by three hundred and seventy-six FR Mk I's, officially designated as fighter-reconnaissance aircraft and carrying ASH detection radar. During production of the Mk I series, modifications introduced included a revised front cockpit hood, fully faired gun barrels and, from the four hundred and seventy-first aircraft onward, substitution of the 1,765 hp Griffon XII engine. Meanwhile, thirty-seven examples had been completed of a night fighter model, the NF Mk II, with twin leading-edge fairings housing the scanners of their AI radar, and a slightly longer fuselage. They were superseded by the NF Mk I, with an improved radar carried in a single under-nose pod but otherwise structurally similar to the other Mk I's. The proposed Firefly III was abandoned, after one aircraft had been tested with a Griffon 61 series engine, in favour of the Mk IV which, with a 2,330 hp Griffon 72, was flown in 1944. This version was further modified in 1945, but did not enter service until after the war had ended.

56 & 57 Supermarine Spitfire and Seafire

One of the select few combat aeroplanes to become a legend in its own lifetime, the Spitfire and its naval counterpart, the Seafire, appeared in more than forty major variants* during its service career,

and remained in continuous production throughout the entire period of World War 2 – the only Allied warplane to do so. The Spitfire's designer, Reginald J. Mitchell, had ideas of his own regarding the ideal configuration for a single-seat fighter, and his design, which was to become the Spitfire, was so clearly superior to the F.5/34 Specification to which it had been submitted that an entirely new Specification (F.37/34) was drafted to cover the prototype's manufacture. This machine (K 5054), powered by a 990 hp Rolls-Royce Merlin C engine, flew for the first time on 5 March 1936, and two substantial contracts for the fighter were placed in 1936–37. Delivery of the first Spitfire I's, to No 19 Squadron, began in August 1938, and by 3 September 1939 nine squadrons were fully equipped with Spitfires and the total orders were in excess of two thousand. One thousand five hundred and sixty-six Spitfire I's (1,030 hp Merlin II or III) were eventually built, this being the principal model in service during the Battle of Britain. It was during the career of this version that two of the three basic Spitfire wing configurations became established. The original wing, mounting eight 0·303 in Browning machine-guns, became known as the 'A' wing; the 'B' wing mounted four Brownings with two 20 mm Hispano cannon. The 'C' wing, first introduced into ser-

* The various Mk numbers were not always built in chronological order, and some changes in Mk number occurred; the description here has therefore been somewhat simplified, for reasons of space, to avoid unnecessary confusion.

vice on the Mk VC, was a 'universal' wing capable of mounting four machine-guns, two cannon, or one cannon and two machine-guns in each half. The Spitfire II, with 1,175 hp Merlin XII, entered service late in 1940; nine hundred and twenty were built, some of which were later converted to Mk V's. Only one experimental Mk III (1,280 hp Merlin XX) was completed, the chronology then continuing with two hundred and twenty-nine Mk IV's (actually produced after the Mk V) equipped for photographic reconnaissance. The first really large-scale model was the Spitfire V, which began to enter service in March 1941. Six thousand four hundred and seventy-nine examples of this version were completed. In addition to the standard elliptical-pattern wings, Spitfires were modified for low-level fighting with 'clipped' wingtips, and for high-altitude roles with pointed tip extensions. First in the latter category were the pressurised Mk VI (one hundred built) and Mk VII interceptors (one hundred and forty built), the Mk VII having a redesigned fuselage and a 1,710 hp Merlin 64 engine. The Mk VII was the first variant to exceed 400 mph (644 km/hr) in level flight. The Spitfire VIII appeared in 1943 in high-, intermediate- and low-level forms, a total of one thousand six hundred and fifty-eight being completed, but it was preceded in 1942 by the Mk IX. This was, in essence, the Spitfire VC airframe with a Merlin 60-series engine installed. Production of the Mk IX totalled

five thousand six hundred and sixty five. The Mk IX appeared with standard, clipped and extended wings, and introduced a fourth variation: the 'E' wing, with one Hispano and one 0·50 in Browning in each half. The sixteen Mk X built, and four hundred and seventy one Mk XI, were photo-reconnais sance variants. Another major stage in the Spitfire's evolution came in 1943 with the Mk XII (one hundred built), in which the Merlin engine was replaced by a 1,735 hp Griffon III or IV and the vertical tail area was increased. The Mk XIV including the clipped-wing FR Mk XIVE (total of nine hundred and fifty-seven completed), were based upon the Mk VIII, locally strength ened to take a 2,050 hp Griffon 65 engine. This model was used successfully against the V1 flying bombs in 1944, and was also the first aircraft to destroy one of the new Me 262 jet fighters in aerial combat. The Spitfire XVI, which entered service in 1944, was a ground-attack model basically simi lar to the earlier Mk IX, except that it employed a Packard-built Merlin 266 engine; one thousand and fifty four were built. The Spitfire XIX was an unarmed photo-reconnais sance derivative of the Mk XIV with a Griffon 65 or 66 engine; two hundred and forty-five were built serving both in Europe and in the Far East. Variants which did not become operational before the war's end, but which kept production going until October 1947, included the Mks XVIII, 21, 22 and 24. Overall Spitfire production totalled twenty thousand three hundred and thirty-four. In addition to their service with the RAF and Commonwealth air forces, many other Spitfires, of various marks, were supplied during the war years to the USAAF, the Soviet Air Force, and the air arms of Egypt, Portugal and Turkey. The Spitfire also enjoyed a successful career at sea. Following the adaptation of the Hurricane (q.v.) for shipboard operation, deck-landing trials were conducted aboard HMS *Illustrious* late in 1941 with a standard Spitfire VB equipped with catapult points and an arrester hook. An order was then placed for some one hundred and sixty-six similar conversions, which were named Seafire IB. The first of these entered Fleet Air Arm service (with No 807 Squadron) in mid-1942, to be followed by three hundred and seventy-two Seafire IIC's – built from the outset as Seafires and based on the Spitfire VC. A considerable improvement over these interim versions was evident in the Mk III of 1943, powered by various marks of Merlin engine and the first Seafire to incorporate wing folding. One thousand two hundred and twenty Seafire III's were completed, many of them fitted with photo-reconnaissance cameras. Installation of the Griffon engine was pursued under Specification N.4/43, the first variant with this powerplant (a 1,850 hp Griffon VI) being the Seafire XV which appeared in 1944. Three hundred and ninety Seafire XV's were completed, entering service in May 1945; but this model was still

working up for employment in the Pacific theatre when the war in the Far East ended. Post-war Seafires in service included the Mks XVII, 45, 46 and 47, some of which were operational during the Korean War of 1950–53.

58 Curtiss P-40 Warhawk

Although not an outstanding combat aeroplane, the Curtiss P-40 served with the USAAF and other Allied air forces in every operational theatre of World War 2, was built in considerable numbers and proved to be highly adaptable to a variety of tasks. Moreover, it had the added advantage of being available in quantity at a time when more sophisticated and more famous wartime fighters were still in the early stages of development or production. Its design originated in 1937, as a development of the radial-engined P-36 (Hawk 75), powered by the new Allison V-1710 Vee-type engine. The prototype XP-40, a converted P-36A airframe, was flown in October 1938, and in April 1939 an order was placed for five hundred and twenty-four production P-40's. This was later reduced to two hundred, to permit Curtiss to meet an order for one hundred and forty similar machines placed by the French government. In the event, the French aircraft were diverted to the RAF in 1940, who named them Tomahawk I. Most of these, due to their poor armament (two 0·30 in guns) were relegated to the Middle East or to Army Co-operation units. The RAF's Tomahawk IIA (one hundred and ten received) corresponded with the P-40B for the USAAF (one hundred and thirty-one) and had two additional wing-mounted guns, self-sealing fuel tanks and extra armour protection. One hundred P-40B's were diverted from a British order to supply the American Volunteer Group in China. Two more wing guns, making six guns in all, characterised the P-40C, the USAAF receiving one hundred and ninety-three and the RAF nine hundred and thirty as the Tomahawk IIB. The first substantial redesign appeared in the P-40D of 1941, which had a shorter nose, minus the nose guns, and a deeper radiator beneath an Allison V-1710-39 engine. The four wing guns were raised to 0·50 in calibre, and provision existed for bombs to be carried beneath the fuselage and wings. Only twenty-two P-40D's went to the USAAF, but five hundred and sixty were allocated to the RAF, which gave them the new name Kittyhawk I. The USAAF preferred the P-40E, with six wing guns; it ordered eight hundred and twenty of this model, and another fifteen hundred became Kittyhawk IA's. Several were also delivered to the RAAF and RCAF. Installation of Packard-built Merlin engines produced the P-40F, one thousand three hundred and eleven of which were built; one hundred were supplied to the USSR and others to the Free French Air Force (FAFL), but planned delivery of P-40F's to the RAF as Kittyhawk II's did not materialise. The RAF was, however, allocated twenty-one P-40K's and six hundred P-40M's

(Kittyhawk III) and five hundred and eighty-six P-40N's (Kittyhawk IV). US production included thirteen hundred P-40K's, with slightly increased fin area; seven hundred P-40L's (similar to the F but with only four guns); and four thousand two hundred and nineteen P-40N's. The N model had the four guns and other weight-saving attributes of the F and L, combined with a 1,360 hp V-1710-81 engine. In 1944, many former F and L models had their Merlin engines replaced by Allisons and were converted as P-40R advanced trainers. Production ended in December 1944 after a grand total of thirteen thousand seven hundred and thirty-eight P-40 series aircraft had been produced.

59 Airspeed Oxford

The origin of the Oxford twin-engined trainer lay in the 8-passenger Envoy III, which served with the King's Flight of the RAF in the mid-1930s. From this was developed a version known as the Convertible Envoy, seven of which were built for the South African Air Force with a hand-operated dorsal turret mounting a single machine-gun. Major differences discernible in the Oxford I, which first flew in January 1937, were wings of increased span and area, a modified fuselage nose and fully cowled Cheetah IX engines. Delivery of the Oxford I, to the Central Flying School, began in November 1937, and some three hundred were in RAF service by the outbreak of World War 2. Initially, the Oxford I was equipped to provide training in navigation, bombing and gunnery; the advent of powered turrets in wartime combat aircraft rendered the Oxford's hand-operated turret extinct, although it normally remained in position on most Oxford I's in service. By 3 September 1939 there were also in service over seventy examples of the Oxford II, produced for pilot training and lacking the dorsal turret. Several Oxford II's were later used for ambulance duties. The Oxford III and the Gipsy Queen-engined Oxford IV were projects only. The final production model was the Oxford V, whose performance was somewhat improved by the introduction of 450 hp Pratt & Whitney R-985-AN-5 Wasp Junior engines. Total Oxford production, by Airspeed, de Havilland, Percival and Standard Motors, reached eight thousand seven hundred and fifty-one. Among these, the Mks I and II predominated, although many of them were later converted to Mk V standard with American engines. Oxfords were used as trainers in every major Commonwealth country, and as ambulances in the Middle East.

50 Henschel Hs 129

The 1938 RLM specification that resulted in the Hs 129 was prompted by the need, revealed during the Spanish Civil War, for a specialised close support and ground-attack aeroplane. Dipl-Ing Nicholaus of Henschel designed the Hs 129 around the use of twin Argus As 410 engines, three prototypes being completed. The first of these was flown in the spring of 1939, and

in 1940 a small pre-series batch of Hs 129A-o's were sent to a *Luftwaffe* trials unit for evaluation. Pilots' reports were highly unfavourable, chiefly due to the aircraft's inadequate power, and were sufficiently damning to prevent the Argus-engined Hs 129A from entering production. The existing Hs 129A-o's were not, evidently, too unsatisfactory to pass on to the Rumanian Air Force, which used them for some months on the Russian Front. Meanwhile, Herr Nicholaus's team produced an alternative design, known originally by the project number P.76, but this was rejected by the RLM, which directed instead that the Hs 129A be adapted to take captured French Ghome-Rhône 14M radial engines. Thus re-engined, and with cockpit and other internal modifications, the type became known in 1941 as the Hs 129B. The Hs 129B-1, following a batch of seven pre-series Hs 129B-o's, entered production in autumn 1941, and became operational with *Luftwaffe* units in the Crimea early in 1942. Later, the Hs 129B appeared in numbers in North Africa, being employed primarily as an anti-tank aircraft in both theatres. Several B-1 sub-types were produced, with various combinations of armament. Standard equipment, as installed in the B-1/R1, comprised two 20 mm MG 151 cannon and two 7·9 mm MG 17 machine-guns, with provision for a small external bomb load. Without bombs, and with a fixed ventral 30 mm MK 101 cannon, it was designated B-1/R2; the B-1/R3 had the big cannon replaced by a ventral tray of four more MG 17's; the B-1/R4 and B-1/R5 each carried the standard quota of guns, but with a more varied bomb load and photo-reconnaissance camera respectively. The B-1/R2 was notably successful in the anti-tank role, and prompted the evolution of the all-gun B-2 series. The B-2/R1 was similar to the B-1/R1 except that 13 mm MG 131's replaced the MG 17's; to this the B-2/R2 added a 30 mm MK 103 cannon; while the B-2/R3 discarded the two MG 131's in favour of two more MG 151's (making four in all) and a 37 mm cannon. Final version was the B-2/R4, with a huge 75 mm ventral cannon whose muzzle projected nearly 8 ft (2·4 m) ahead of the aircraft's nose. A total of eight hundred and sixty-six Hs 129B's were built before production ceased in the summer of 1944.

61   Bristol Beaufighter

The Beaufighter originated in 1938 as a private-venture design, based upon the wings, rear fuselage and tail unit of the Beaufort torpedo bomber. The prototype (R 2052) first flew on 17 July 1939, by which time Specification F.17/39 had been issued to cover a handsome initial order for three hundred of these pug-nosed fighters. By the end of May 1940 three other prototypes were flying, and the first small batch of Mk IF production aircraft was accepted by the RAF in 1940; first combat success was by aircraft of No 640 Squadron in November 1940. With their 10-gun armament and airborne interception radar, the early Beaufighters were the most potent night fighters in production and service, and by the end of 1940 they were performing also as day fighters in the Western Desert. In the spring of 1941, No 143 Squadron of Coastal Command became the first unit to operate the Mk IC, a coastal protection and anti-shipping version otherwise similar to the Mk IF and also powered by 1,590 hp Hercules XI engines. Nine hundred and fourteen Beaufighter I's were built. To avoid undue drain on the output of Hercules engines, orders were also placed for the Merlin-engined Mk II, two prototypes of which had been flown in 1940. Four hundred and fifty production Mk IIF's were built, with the 1,280 hp Merlin XX as their standard powerplant. Most of them served as night fighters in the UK, but a number were delivered to the Fleet Air Arm. A slight tendency toward instability already noticed in the Beaufighter I became even more noticeable in the Mk II with its longer Merlin nacelles. It was cured, after some experiment by giving the tailplane 12 degrees of dihedral, a modification that became standard on all aircraft of the type. The Mks III, IV and V were experimental variants, the next large-scale model being the Mk VI, produced, like the Mk I, as the VIF and VIC for Fighter and Coastal Command respectively. The main difference was the return to a more powerful Hercules engine, giving the Beaufighter enhanced performance, including the ability to carry a small bomb load. The dorsal

Vickers K gun for the observer first appeared on this version, one thousand eight hundred and thirty of which were built. (Sixty of these were completed as ITF = Interim Torpedo Fighters. The torpedo-carrying Beaufighters are described in the *Bombers, Patrol and Transport Aircraft 1939–45* volume). A number of Beaufighter VIF's served with the USAAF in 1943, and others were fitted with the AI radar nose 'thimble' that later characterised the TF Mk X. British production of Beaufighters (all variants) totalled five thousand five hundred and sixty-two, and ended in September 1945.

62 Junkers Ju 88

In parallel with the Ju 88A bomber series (see *Bombers, Patrol and Transport Aircraft 1939–45*), Junkers also pursued the development of the basic airframe as a 'heavy' fighter, for which its speed and sturdy construction rendered it particularly suitable. This emerged as the Ju 88C, of which the first version was the C-2, a conversion of the Ju 88A-1, with a solid' nose mounting three MG 17 machine-guns and a 20 mm MG FF cannon, and a single aft-firing MG 15 gun. It entered service with NJG.1 late in 1940, being followed by small batches of the C-4, which utilised the extended-span wings of the Ju 88A-4 bomber, and the C-5. Nose armament was increased by two more cannon in the C-6, with Jumo 211J engines and the rear-firing MG 15 replaced by an MG 131 gun. Final C sub-type was the C-7 which, like the C-6, operated as

both a day and a night fighter. The next night-fighter model was the Ju 88G, which utilised the same angular vertical tail as the Ju 188 bomber and carried improved Lichtenstein radar. The G series appeared from mid-1944, principal sub-types being the G-1 (BMW 801D engines), G-6a and G-6b (BMW 801G), G-6c (Jumo 213A) and G-7 (Jumo 213E-1). A small batch of H-2 'heavy' fighters was built, and the Ju 88 fighter variants then came to an end with the Ju 88R, produced in R-1 and R-2 forms for day and night fighting respectively. A specialised version also appeared, for service primarily on the Russian Front, in general ground-attack/anti-tank configuration. This variant was the Ju 88P, with either a 75 mm cannon (in the P-1) or two 37 mm cannon (in the P-2) mounted in the nose. Of the overall Ju 88 production total of fourteen thousand six hundred and seventy-six aircraft (not counting prototypes), slightly over three thousand nine hundred were completed as fighter or ground-attack variants.

63 Kawasaki Ki-45 Toryu (Dragon Killer)

The Ki-45, known by the Allied wartime code name 'Nick', originated in the earlier Kawasaki Ki-38 evolved to a 1937 JAAF requirement for a long-range escort fighter. However, so extensive were the modifications required by the JAAF that a new designation was allotted. Six Ki-45 prototypes were built initially, the first being flown in January 1939. Due to problems encountered with both the landing gear and the Ha-20B engines during trials, three of the prototypes resumed flight testing in July 1940 re-engined with Mitsubishi Ha-25's. In slightly enlarged and modified form, the fighter eventually entered production in September 1941 as the Ki-45-Kai. A second Kawasaki factory joined the production programme in August 1942, by which time the Ha-102 engine had become the standard powerplant. With this engine and the original armament the fighter was now designated Ki-45-Kai-A; the Kai-B initially had one 12·7 mm and one 37 mm gun in the front fuselage; the Kai-C and -D differed in internal equipment only. The Ki-45 was by now being used increasingly as a night fighter, and some mounted a 50 mm or 75 mm weapon for anti-shipping missions. An eventual fourteen prototypes and one thousand six hundred and eighty-seven production Toryus were completed by Kawasaki between 1939 and 1945, the type becoming operational early in 1942 as escort fighter, patrol and anti-shipping aircraft. The Ki-45 was used extensively in the suicide role, being the first JAAF type to figure in this form of warfare during World War 2. It was also one of the most effective night fighters used in the home defence of Japan in 1944–45. The projected Ki-45-II, with 1,500 hp Ha-112-II engines, was converted from December 1942 to become the single-seat Ki-96, three prototypes of which were completed. The first of these was flown in September 1943, but the project was later abandoned by the JAAF and several Ki-96 components were later used in completing prototypes of the Kawasaki Ki-102.

64 Nakajima J1N

The Nakajima J1N was evolved originally as a multi-seat escort fighter and attack aircraft, and was entered, together with a Mitsubishi design, to meet a JNAF requirement issued in June 1938. The Mitsubishi entry was later withdrawn and the Nakajima prototype designed by K. Nakamura, flew for the first time in May 1941. The J1N proved somewhat difficult to handle and manoeuvre, and the remote control mechanism for the rear gun barbettes gave trouble, but it's general performance was satisfactory enough, and the JNAF decided to adopt it instead for a reconnaissance role. With the rear guns deleted, and powered by 1,130 hp Sakae 21 engines, it entered production in the summer of 1942 as the J1N1-C Model 11, and began to reach JNAF units in the Solomon Islands toward the end of the year. Requests from the combat areas led the Japanese Navy to agree in March 1943 to the modification of two J1N1-C's as night fighters, with two pairs of 20 mm cannon aft of the cockpit, to fire at a 30-degree angle above and below the rear fuselage. Following the successful operational use of these two machines, the 2-seat J1N1-S Model 11 night fighter entered production this receiving the name Gekko (Moonlight). The Allied code name for both J1N models, was 'Irving'.

Some J1N1-C's were converted, as an interim measure, to J1N1-F fighters with one 20 mm cannon in a hand-operated dorsal turret. Later Gekkos were equipped with airborne interception radar and deployed against the B-29's attacking Japanese targets, but they lacked the speed or performance at altitude to be fully effective. Some, with an underwing bomb load, were used in the attack role, and the J1N was also proposed (though never used) as a torpedo carrier. Including prototypes, Nakajima built a total of four hundred and seventy-seven of all versions.

65 Tachikawa Ki-54

The Ki-54, which appeared in prototype form in the summer of 1940, was employed as a civilian transport by several Japanese commercial operators before the beginning of the war in the Pacific. It possessed a better performance than other Japanese aircraft in its class by virtue of its clean lines, fully retractable main landing gear and variable-pitch propellers, although it exhibited a tendency toward nose-heaviness when landing. The type was produced as an advanced trainer for the JAAF, being equipped to provide instruction in bombing and gunnery techniques as well as pilot and navigator training. Later in the war a version known as the Model C appeared for the troop transport role, being furnished with seats for up to nine passengers. In many respects the career of the Ki-54 (code named 'Hickory' by the Allies) paralleled that of the Air-speed Oxford, although it was built in considerably smaller numbers; about one thousand two hundred were completed by Tachikawa prior to the end of the war. Many of these were used in the suicide role during 1944–45.

66 Potez 63

Evolved to a 1934 specification for a 3-seat strategic fighter, the Potez 63 was designed by MM Coroller and Delaruelle, the -01 prototype flying for the first time on 25 April 1936. In general appearance it bore a superficial resemblance to its German contemporary, the Messerschmitt Bf 110, a fact which contributed to the loss of many Potez fighters during combat in World War 2. The Hispano-Suiza-engined first prototype was later redesignated Potez 630-01, to distinguish it from the second machine (631-01), which had Gnome-Rhône engines. In May 1937 the French Air Ministry ordered ten evaluation machines which included representatives of both types, together with examples of the Potez 633 (light bomber configuration), 637 (reconnaissance and Army co-operation) and 639 (attack bomber). In June 1937 the Potez company became part of the new SNCA du Nord, from which was ordered eighty Potez 630's and ninety Potez 631's, the latter figure including ten with dual controls for conversion training. Orders were placed in 1938 for one hundred and twenty-five Potez 633's for the *Armée de l'Air*, plus export batches for Greece (twenty-four) and Rumania (forty); a manufacturing licence was also granted to Avia in Czechoslovakia, but none were built in that country. Only eleven of the Greek and twenty-one of the Rumanian 633's had been delivered by August 1939, when delivery of the remainder was halted by the French government. Production of the Potez 631 by this time had reached two hundred and ten for the *Armée de l'Air*. Also completed were sixty Potez 637's, but this was essentially an interim service model pending availability of the Potez 63.11, a much-redesigned development which was first flown on 31 December 1938. This differed principally in the design of the front fuselage, and an initial order had been placed for one hundred and forty-five for the armed reconnaissance role. Nearly seventeen hundred more were ordered in 1939. Production continued under German direction after the occupation of France, and the eventual total of Potez 63.11's completed appears to have been in the region of nine hundred. Variants of the Potez 63 series served with units of the *Luftwaffe* and the Vichy Air Force, as well as with the FAFL, in Europe and North Africa.

67 Heinkel He 219 Uhu(Owl)

After an initial lack of interest when proposals for this multi-purpose fighter were first submitted to it in August 1940, the RLM authorised Heinkel, late in 1941, to begin detailed design work on the project. The first He 219 prototype was flown on 15 November 1942, powered by two 1,750 hp DB 603A engines, and

underwent armament trials during the following month. An initial order was placed for one hundred production aircraft, and this figure was increased to three hundred by the time tooling-up began in April 1943. About twenty pre-series He 219A-0's had been completed by the summer, and were followed by forty examples of the He 219A-2 (the A-1 having been abandoned). The A-2 was a 2-seat model; proposals for the 3-seat A-3 bomber and the high-altitude reconnaissance A-4 sub-types were not adopted. Production thus continued with the A-5, A-6 and A-7; most of these were powered by variants of the DB 603 engine, but Jumo 213E's were installed in the A-7/R5 and Jumo 222's in the A-7/R6. The A-5 was a 3-seater and carried additional internal fuel. Total production of the He 219A-series aircraft was two hundred and sixty-eight, and these, together with some twenty prototype or pre-production machines and a few 2-seat He 219B-2's (developed from the A-6) were the only models to serve operationally with the *Luftwaffe*. Prototype airframes were completed of the He 219C-1 night fighter and C-2 fighter-bomber, but when VE-day arrived these still awaited delivery of their Jumo 222 engines. The C series were to have carried a 4-man crew, the additional member manning a tail turret with four MG 131 machine-guns.

68 Dornier Do 217

In an attempt to overcome a severe shortage of specialised night fighters, the *Luftwaffe* in 1942 initiated the conversion of large numbers of Dornier 217 bombers to fulfil this function. Fundamentally, the airframe conversion entailed replacing the bulbous, glazed nose of the bomber with a more streamlined 'solid' fairing containing additional guns. First version selected for conversion was the Do 217E-2. A total of one hundred and fifty-seven E-2's underwent modification, after which they were redesignated Do 217J-1 or -2. The former was an intruder version, retaining a reduced bomb-carrying capability, while the J-2 night fighter had the bomb bay faired over and was equipped with Lichtenstein airborne interception radar. Both mounted four 20 mm cannon and four 7·9 mm machine-guns in the nose, and had provision for one 13 mm gun in a ventral position, in addition to the dorsal armament. In 1943 the J series began to be replaced by the Lichtenstein-equipped Do 217N series, powered by DB 603A in-line engines and converted from the M series bombers. The N-1 and N-2 were both night fighters, and were otherwise generally similar to the J-2 except that the N-2 had no ventral gun. Fifty conversions from M to N were carried out. The non-fighter Do 217 models are described in the *Bombers, Patrol and Transport Aircraft 1939–45* volume.

69 Westland Whirlwind

The Whirlwind was one of several British wartime aircraft to fall victim to the vicissitudes of the Rolls-Royce Peregrine engine; but for this its service career might well have been more significant, for it was a fast, well-armed design with excellent manoeuvrability and first-class flying qualities. It was designed by William Petter to Specification F.37/35, the first of two prototypes (L 6844) being flown on 11 October 1938. Production was ordered three months later, but delays in the supply of Peregrine engines caused the first deliveries of Whirlwind I fighters (to No 263 Squadron) to be put back until July 1940. Several accidents, due to rather poor forward vision in the landing attitude and the fighter's high landing speed, delayed the equipment of the second Whirlwind squadron (No 137) until November 1941, and these remained the only two RAF squadrons to employ the type. The Whirlwind's performance was particularly good at low altitude, a factor that contributed to its employment during the latter half of 1942 in the fighter-bomber role; previously it had been employed as an interceptor or escort fighter. But in January 1942, following the abandonment of Peregrine production, manufacture of the Whirlwind also ceased. One hundred and sixteen were built, including the two prototypes.

70 De Havilland Mosquito

Although conceived as a fast day bomber, the D.H.98 Mosquito had too good a turn of speed for its potential as a fighter to pass unnoticed, and the third of the three prototypes (W 4052), which first flew on 15 May 1941, was completed to a night-fighter configuration with AI Mk IV radar in a 'solid' nose.

Four hundred and sixty-six Mosquito Mk II's were subsequently built, the first deliveries being made to No 157 Squadron in January 1942 as replacements for the Douglas A-20 Havoc. Ninety-seven Mk II's were later converted to NF Mk XII's with centrimetric AI Mk VIII radar, followed by two hundred and seventy NF XIII's, the production counterpart of the Mk XII. On these subsequent radar-carrying night fighters the nose machine-guns were omitted. Other specialist night fighter models included the Mks XV, XVII (one hundred conversions from Mk II), and XIX (two hundred and twenty built), the two last-named having AI Mk X radar of US manufacture. The most numerous version of all, however, was the Mosquito Mk VI, of which two thousand seven hundred and eighteen were built during and after the war. The first Mk VI was a converted Mk II (HJ 662), first flown in its new form in February 1943. Carrying the standard fighter armament, the Mk VI was able to carry two 250 lb or 500 lb (113 or 227 kg) bombs in the rear of the bomb bay, with two additional bombs or auxiliary fuel tanks beneath the outer wing sections. It entered service with No 418 Squadron in the spring of 1943. An alternative load comprised eight 60 lb (27 kg) rocket projectiles, and Mk VI's so equipped entered service with Coastal Command early in 1944 for anti-shipping strike duties. They had actually been preceded by a small batch of twenty-seven FB XVIII's produced by converting the standard FB VI to mount a 57 mm cannon in the nose. Principal Canadian and Australian counterparts to the FB VI were the FB 26 and FB 40 with Packard-built Merlin engines. Whether as a bomber, day or night fighter, reconnaissance or intruder, the Mosquito in its many guises served in all operational theatres of the war, including the Pacific area from early 1944. Three hundred and forty-eight examples were also built of a trainer variant, the T Mk III; most of these were delivered to the RAF, but some were sold abroad and a few were also supplied to the Fleet Air Arm. The other non-fighter variants are described in the *Bombers, Patrol and Transport Aircraft 1939–45* volume.

71 Messerschmitt Me 210 and Me 410 Hornisse (Hornet)

The Me 210 was designed as a potential successor to the Bf 110, and RLM approval of the project in 1937 was followed on 2 September 1939 by the first flight of the twin-finned Me 210V1 prototype. This aircraft showed marked instability in flight, and attempts to remedy this resulted in a large-area single fin and rudder being introduced on the second machine. This still did not eliminate all the Me 210's control problems, but the RLM had committed itself to a substantial order for one thousand aircraft of this type before the first prototype had flown. The three production models – the Me 210A-1, A-2 and B-1, were all similarly powered, with 1,395 hp DB 601F engines; the A-2 was fitted with external bomb racks, while the B-1 had the two MG 17 guns deleted and carried two aerial reconnaissance cameras. In April 1942, however, the RLM halted production of the Me 210. It was later resumed for a brief period, but the final total completed in Germany was only three hundred and fifty-two, plus one hundred and eight built under licence in Hungary with DB 605 engines. In the search for a replacement type, the RLM passed over the pressurised Me 310 project in favour of a simpler derivative, the Me 410, which was also powered by DB 603A engines. Known as the *Hornisse*, the Me 410 entered production late in 1942. By 1944 a total of one thousand one hundred and twenty-one had been manufactured. Several A and B sub-types were produced, with armament or equipment variations, for service as 'heavy' fighters, bomber destroyers and photographic reconnaissance aircraft. The Me 410A-3 and B-3 had bulged bomb-bay fairings containing three aerial cameras.

72   Messerschmitt Bf 110

The Bf 110 was the second production warplane designed by Prof Willy Messerschmitt after joining the Bayerische Flugzeugwerke AG, and was evolved in response to an RLM specification of early 1934 for a long-range escort fighter and *Zerstörer* (destroyer) aircraft. Three prototypes were completed with DB 600 engines, and the first of these was flown on 12 May 1936. The second, delivered early in the next year to the *Luftwaffe* for service

trials, was received with mixed feelings. It was fast for a relatively heavy twin-engined machine, but was also heavy on the controls and less manoeuvrable than was desired. Four pre-series Bf 110A-0's were ordered, and these, due to the comparative scarcity of DB 600 engines, were fitted instead with 610 hp Jumo 210B units. These proved clearly inadequate, and were succeeded in the spring of 1938 by two Bf 110B-0 aircraft with 690 hp DB 600A engines to carry out trials for the initial Bf 110B-1 production series. Plans to evaluate the B-1 operationally in the Spanish Civil War were forestalled when that conflict was resolved before it was ready for service. Thus, the first model to go into active service was the Bf 110C, in which increased power was provided by the use of DB 601A engines. Other refinements appearing in the C model included squared-off wingtips to improve the manoeuvrability, and a modified crew enclosure. The Bf 110C entered service in 1939, over five hundred of this model being on the *Luftwaffe*'s strength by the end of that year. Some were produced for the fighter-bomber and reconnaissance roles, and the Bf 110 was employed primarily in ground-attack manoeuvres during the invasion of Poland. Hence it was not until it was fully exposed as a fighter, in the Battle of Britain, that its shortcomings in that capacity became apparent. Losses then became so heavy that the Luftwaffe was obliged to send Bf 109's with the bomber formations to protect their Bf 110 escorts. Production of the C model continued, latterly with 1,200 hp DB 601N engines, but many of the earlier machines were withdrawn to such second-line duties as glider towing. Attempts to boost the aircraft's range resulted in the Bf 110D, produced both as a fighter (D-0 and D-1) and as a fighter-bomber (D-2 and D-3), but by mid-1941 most of the C and D versions were operational only in the Middle East or on the Eastern Front. The more versatile Bf 110E (DB 601N) and Bf 110F (DB 601F) appeared later that year, variants including the rocket-firing F-2 and the F-4 night fighter. By late 1942, when it became apparent that the Me 210 was not going to be a satisfactory replacement for its predecessor, Bf 110 production was stepped up again and the Bf 110G was introduced. This followed the pattern of earlier series, including the G-4 night fighter with 1,475 hp DB 605B engines, two or four 20 mm cannon and four 7·9 mm machine-guns. The four-seat Bf 110G-4/R3 was the first variant to incorporate Lichtenstein SN-2 airborne interception radar. The Bf 110H series, differing chiefly in carrying even heavier armament, was produced in parallel with the G series, and was the last production model. Total Bf 110 production, in all versions, was approximately six thousand one hundred and fifty, and ended early in 1945.

73   Siebel Si 204D

The Si 204D was developed in 1940–41 by Dipl-Ing Fecher from the pre-war Fh 104 *Hallore* and Si 204A

medium transports, from which it chief external difference was the replacement of the original 'stepped' solid nose by a bulbous, fully glazed section forming a continuous contour with the remainder of the front fuselage. The Si 204A was powered by two 360 hp Argus As 410A engines, and some served with the *Luftwaffe* in the light transport or liaison roles. The more powerful Si 204D, flown in prototype form in 1941, succeeded the Focke-Wulf Fw 58 as the standard *Luftwaffe* aircrew trainer and could be furnished to accommodate five trainees in addition to the 2-man crew. It remained in service until the end of World War 2, latterly for radar as well as navigation training. Most of its manufacture was undertaken in German-held factories in Czechoslovakia and France. The SNCA du Centre continued to build the Si 204D, in slightly modified form, as the NC 701 (military) and NC 702 Martinet (civil) after the war, and Aero in Czechoslovakia also built a substantial number of post-war examples as military and civil transports.

74   Fokker G.I

Before the G.I prototype had flown, it was exhibited at the 1936 *Salon de l'Aéronautique* in Paris, where its formidable armament – one arrangement offered eight machine-guns clustered in the nose and a ninth at the rear – quickly earned it the nickname *Le Faucheur* (the Grim Reaper). It was evolved by Fokker as a private venture 2-seat design for a bomber interceptor, and the prototype (X-2) first flew on 16 March 1937, powered by two 750 hp Hispano-Suiza 80-02 radial engines. In November 1937 thirty-six examples were ordered by the Dutch government of the G.IA, a slightly modified version with 830 hp Bristol Mercury VIII engines and provision in four aircraft for a third crew member. A slightly smaller 2-seat model, with 750 hp Twin Wasp Junior engines, was offered for export as the G.IB. For the latter, Denmark sought a manufacturing licence, and orders were received from Estonia (for nine), Finland (twenty-six), Sweden (eighteen, to be fitted with Swedish-built Bofors guns) and Spain. When Holland was invaded on 10 May 1940 twelve of the Finnish G.IB's were still at Schiphol, their delivery having been halted upon the outbreak of war. They were unarmed, but enough guns were taken from other nearby aircraft to fit three G.IB's with four guns each and fly them against the *Luftwaffe*. The remaining fourteen Finnish aircraft were completed after the German occupation and employed by the *Luftwaffe* as operational trainers. Meanwhile, delivery of the G.IA to the Dutch Air Force's 3rd and 4th Fighter Groups had started in July 1939, and twenty-three were operational when the invasion began. Several were destroyed on the ground before they could take part in the fighting, but those that survived gave a good account of themselves in the five days of bitter fighting that ensued. At the end of this, only one G.IA was left, but in this machine two

senior Fokker pilots managed to escape later to Britain.

75 Lockheed P-38 Lightning

If one aeroplane were to be chosen from those taking part in World War 2 to epitomise the successful realisation of the long-range tactical fighter, few would dispute the claims of Lockheed's 'fork-tailed devil', the P-38 Lightning. Work on its design was started early in 1937, to meet an exacting USAAC requirement. The Lockheed Model 22 was a clear winner of the competition, and in June 1937 one prototype, designated XP-38, was ordered. This machine (37-457) first flew on 27 January 1939, followed on 16 September 1940 by the first of thirteen YP-38 evaluation aircraft with more powerful V-1710 engines and a nose armament of four machine-guns and a 37 mm cannon. Delivery of production P-38's began in the summer of 1941; thirty were built, one being modified to an XP-38A with a pressurised cabin. The next production model was the P-38D, thirty-six of which were manufactured with self-sealing fuel tanks and minor airframe modifications. The name Lightning was originally bestowed by the RAF, which had ordered the type in 1940, but initial deliveries were restricted to three Lightning I's (with non-supercharged engines) and a contract for five hundred and twenty-four Lightning II's was subsequently cancelled. The remaining one hundred and forty Mk I's were repossessed (as the P-322) by the USAAF, which acquired the Mk

II's built for Britain as well; many of these were later converted to P-38F or G standard. Meanwhile, the USAAF's own next choice, the P-38E, had entered production. Two hundred and ten were built, with double the D's ammunition for the nose guns and a 20 mm cannon replacing the heavier weapon. An increase in engine power was the major improvement in the F and G models, thus enabling the Lightning to carry a range of external weapons or supplementary fuel tanks for the first time. Production of five hundred and twenty-seven P-38F's and one thousand and eighty-two P-38G's, with deliveries beginning during 1942, heralded a marked expansion in the Lightning's deployment in the major theatres of the war in Europe, North Africa and the Pacific. A further increase in engine power appeared in 1943 with the P-38H, the first Lightning model to introduce the 'chin' air cooler intakes beneath the spinners. Six hundred and one P-38H's were delivered; the two thousand nine hundred and seventy P-38J's that followed were essentially similar, but an increased internal fuel load raised the endurance of the J model (when carrying drop-tanks as well) to a maximum of 12 hours. An even greater number were built of the rocket-carrying P-38L, with 1,600 hp V-1710-111/113 engines and a maximum speed of 414 mph (666 km/hr). Three thousand eight hundred and ten P-38L's were manufactured by Lockheed; a further two thousand were ordered from Vultee, who had completed

only one hundred and thirteen before the remainder were cancelled at the end of the Pacific war. Lightnings converted for other duties included seventy-five P-38M night fighters (from P-38L), a small number of TP-38L conversion trainers, and the undesignated 'Droop Snoot' and 'Pathfinder' (former P-38J or L models). The Lightning was also the most widely used single photographic reconnaissance aircraft of World War 2, nearly fourteen hundred being converted from P-38E, F, G, H, J and L models and serving with F-4 or F-5 series designations.

76 Saab-21A

Considering that it was the first fighter design undertaken by the Swedish manufacturer, the Saab-21 was remarkable in many respects. It was the only single-engined, twin-boom, pusher-engined fighter to be produced during 1939–45, was the first fighter built in Sweden to have a liquid-cooled engine, and in later years became the only fighter in the world to be produced in both piston-engined and jet-engined forms. Yet the basic configuration was arrived at and presented to the Royal Swedish Air Board within *two weeks* of the Board's March 1941 specification. With the decision to adopt the German DB 605 engine in place of the American Twin Wasp radial originally planned, three prototypes were ordered, and the first of these was flown on 30 July 1943. Thanks to the tricycle landing gear, view from the cockpit for take-off and landing was excellent. The high operational peed of the J 21, as it was designated by the *Flygvapnet*, combined with the rear-mounted propeller, led to the Saab fighter being one of the first in the world to be equipped with an ejection seat for the pilot. Some minor development problems, almost inevitable in such an unorthodox design, delayed delivery of production J 21's until the latter part of 1945. The first machines entered service with F 9 Wing at Gothenburg, and after the first few production aircraft the locally built SFA version of the DB 605B engine was introduced in place of examples imported from Germany. Production of the J 21A continued until 1948, three hundred and one (including three prototypes) being built. Variants included the J 21A-1 (fifty-four built) and J 21A-2 (one hundred and twenty-four built), some of the latter being adapted subsequently as J 21A-2 attack aircraft. The J 21A-3 or A 21A-3 (one hundred and twenty built) had auxiliary wingtip fuel tanks, underwing points for bombs or rocket rails, and provision for a ventral pack of eight additional 13·2 mm machine-guns. The Saab-21B was a proposed development, with a pressurised cockpit and 2,000 hp Griffon engine, but this was discarded in favour of the jet-powered Saab-21R.

77 Bell P-59 Airacomet
The first aeroplane to be designed in the US to acquire experience of the Whittle-type gas turbine engine, the Airacomet project was initiated in the autumn of 1941, the first of three XP-59A prototypes being flown on 1 October 1942. These three machines, bearing for security reasons the designation originally allotted to an entirely different piston-engined Bell fighter project, were powered by two General Electric I-A turbojets, derived from the Whittle W.2B engine. A higher-rated engine, the 1,400 lb (635 kg) st I-16, was installed in the thirteen YP-59A service trials aircraft which followed. Two of these machines were evaluated by the US Navy, and a third was sent to the U.K. in exchange for one of the first Gloster Meteors. In addition to operating problems encountered with the early jet engines, the Airacomet's performance and stability were also below expectations; as a result, the original production order for one hundred aircraft was later reduced, and most of those built were employed for training, engine development and other non-operational duties. Although it took no active part in World War 2, the Airacomet served the primary purpose of establishing the jet fighter concept, paving the way for the P-80 Shooting Star and subsequent fighters with the new form of propulsion. Twenty P-59A's were built with J31-GE-3 engines, and thirty P-59B's with J31-GE-5's, additional internal fuel capacity and detail airframe modifications.

78 Gloster Meteor
Air Ministry Specification F.9/40 was the first official requirement to be promulgated in the UK for a single-seat interceptor powered by

gas turbine engines. From it stemmed W. G. Carter's Gloster Meteor – the first British (and only Allied) jet fighter to achieve operational status during World War 2. The low thrust output of the engines then developed indicated the adoption of a twin-engined configuration, but apart from its radical form of propulsion the Meteor was of completely conventional design. Eight prototypes (of twelve originally ordered) were completed, and it was the fifth of these (DG 206/G) that was used for the first flight on 5 March 1943. Powerplant was two 1,500 lb (680 kg) st Halford H.1 turbojets. Production aircraft – which were to have been named Thunderbolt until that name was adopted for the Republic P-47 – began with twenty Meteor I's powered by 1,700 lb (771 kg) st Rolls-Royce Welland I engines. One of these aircraft was exchanged in 1944 for a Bell YP-59A Airacomet, three others were retained for further development trials, and the remaining sixteen delivered, from July 1944, to the RAF. The first recipient of the new fighters was No 616 Squadron, whose Meteors brought down two V1 flying bombs over southern England on 4 August 1944. One Meteor I was fitted with 2,700 lb (1,225 kg) st de Havilland Goblin I engines as the prototype Meteor II, but no production of this version was undertaken. The first model to be produced in any quantity was the Meteor III, of which two hundred and eighty were completed. The first fifteen of these had Welland engines, the remainder

Derwents, and the final fifteen had lengthened engine nacelles. Two RAF squadrons with the Meteor III were serving with the 2nd Allied Tactical Air Force in Europe during the final weeks of the war, but had no engagements with the Meteor's German counterpart, the Me 262, in aerial combat. One Meteor III, re-engined with 3,500 lb (1,588 kg) st Derwent V's, was flown in July 1945 as prototype for the post-war Mk IV, and all subsequent Meteor development and production also took place after the war had ended.

79 Messerschmitt Me 262

Design of the Me 262 jet fighter, under the Messerschmitt project number 1065, began a year before the outbreak of World War 2. Yet, due to delays in the development and delivery of satisfactory engines, the depredations caused by Allied air attacks, and Hitler's refusal to be advised regarding its most appropriate role, it was six years before the aircraft entered *Luftwaffe* squadron service. Even then, only a fraction of those manufactured before VE-day became operational. A mock-up of the design was completed during the latter half of 1939, examination of which prompted the RLM to order three prototypes in the spring of 1940. These were all completed long before the arrival of their engines and so, to test the basic attributes of the design, the Me 262V1 made its first flight on 4 April 1941 with dummy jet-engine nacelles and a single 700 hp Jumo 210 piston engine mounted in the nose. On 25 November 1941 it attempted to fly with two underwing BMW 003 gas turbines, and still with the nose-mounted Jumo 210 in position. But the first all-jet flight was not made until 18 July 1942, when the third prototype took off under the power of two 1,852 lb (840 kg) st Jumo 004 turbojets. Several more prototypes were completed and used for trials with various armament and equipment installations, and from the fifth machine onward a tricycle landing gear was substituted for the original tailwheel type. A pre-series batch of Me 262A-0's was completed in the spring of 1944, but plans for priority mass-production were seriously affected by Allied air attacks upon Messerschmitt's Regensburg factory, and the planned introduction of the Me 262 into operational service in May 1944 did not take place until the following autumn. The two principal versions which did become operational were the Me 262A-1a Schwalbe (Swallow) interceptor and the Me 262A-2a Sturmvogel (Stormbird). The former was built in a number of sub-types with alternative armament installations; the latter, produced as a result of Hitler's insistence upon developing the aircraft as a bomber, was fitted with external bomb racks. Other variants built included the ground-attack Me 262A-3a and the photo-reconnaissance A-5a. A tandem 2-seat trainer version was designated Me 262B-1a, and one example was completed of a proposed 2-seat night fighter, the B-2a. The few Me 262C models completed before VE-day were fitted with rocket motors in the fuselage to boost the fighter's climb to interception altitudes. Less than six hundred Me 262's had been produced by the end of 1944, but by VE-day the total had risen to one thousand four hundred and thirty-three. Probably less than a quarter of this total saw front-line combat service, and losses among these were quite heavy. In air-to-air combat, the Me 262 never engaged its British counterpart, the Meteor, but many were destroyed by Allied piston-engined Mustang, Thunderbolt, Spitfire and Tempest fighters.

80 Messerschmitt Me 163 Komet (Comet)

Probably the most ingenious and radical German combat aeroplane to serve during World War 2, the Me 163 achieved no small degree of success during the nine months or so that it was in active service, although it reached operational units too late and in numbers too small to affect the ultimate outcome. It was based on the experimental DFS 194, designed in 1938 by Prof Alexander Lippisch and transferred, together with its staff, to the Messerschmitt AG for further development. But for the subsequent clash of personalities between Lippisch and Prof Willy Messerschmitt, and the delay in delivery of its rocket engines in later years, it would almost certainly have been in service much earlier. The first two Me 163 prototypes were flown in the spring of 1941 as unpowered gliders, the Me 163V1 being transferred to Peenemünde later that year to receive its 1,653 lb (750 kg) st HWK R.II rocket motor.

The first rocket-powered flight was made in August 1941, and in trials the fighter soon exhibited speeds of more than 620 mph (1,000 km/hr). Ten unpowered Me 163A's were completed late in 1941 as conversion trainers, and development of the fighter was accelerated. The airframe of the third prototype (for the seventy Me 163B-0 and B-1 production machines ordered) was completed in May 1942, but over a year elapsed before its new engine, the HWK 509A, became available. By then more than half of the original production batch were also complete except for their powerplants. Additional Me 163 production was undertaken by Hans Klemm Flugzeugbau, the overall total being slightly more than three hundred and fifty. The first *Luftwaffe* unit to receive the Me 163B acquired its fighters in June/July 1944, making its operational debut in mid-August against US Eighth Air Force B-17's over Germany. The Komet's spectacular speed, and the element of surprise, resulted in many early successes against Allied bomber formations. However, the definitive version was nearly a ton heavier than its original design weight, necessitating the use of auxiliary booster rockets for take-off, while landings were hazardous in the extreme. All too often the Me 163, landing directly on its fuselage keel-skid and with some of the highly inflammable fuel still left in the tank, would come to a literally comet-like end, with fatal results for its pilot. When the war ended the pressurised and improved Me 163C (HWK 509C motor) had reached the pre-production stage, and a prototype had also been flown of a derivative known first as the Me 163D and later as the Me 263.

INDEX

The reference numbers refer to the illustrations and corresponding text.